Double Standards:
The Selective Outrage of the Left

Double Standards:
The Selective Outrage of the Left

Larry Elder

Creators Publishing
Hermosa Beach, CA

Double Standards: The Selective Outrage of the Left
Copyright © 2017 Creators Publishing
All rights reserved. No part of this book may be reproduced or transmitted in any form or by any means, electronic or mechanical, including photocopying, recording or by any information storage and retrieval system, without permission in writing from the author.

Cover art by Peter Kaminski

CREATORS PUBLISHING
737 3rd St
Hermosa Beach, CA 90254
310-337-7003

Although the author and publisher have made every effort to ensure that the information in this book was correct at press time, the author and publisher do not assume and hereby disclaim any liability to any party for any loss, damage or disruption caused by errors or omissions, whether such errors or omissions result from negligence, accident or any other cause.

ISBN (print): 978-1-945630-65-1
ISBN (ebook): 978-1-945630-64-4

First Edition
Printed in the United States of America
1 3 5 7 9 10 8 6 4 2

Contents

~~~

A Note From the Publisher

Since 1987, Creators has syndicated many of your favorite columns to newspapers. In this digital age, we are bringing collections of those columns to your fingertips. This will allow you to read and reread your favorite columnists, with your own personal digital archive of their work.

Creators Publishing

'Hands Up, Don't Shoot' Activists — and Historical Ignorance

January 1, 2015

What to say about "activists" pushing the "Hands Up, Don't Shoot" "movement," even as police shootings of blacks are actually down 75 percent over the last 45 years? Some protestors, many old enough to know better, say ridiculous things about race relations, like "things have gone backward." Time for perspective.

Booker T. Washington was born a slave. In his autobiography, "Up From Slavery," written in 1901 — just a mere 36 years after the Civil War — Washington wrote:

"As a rule, not only did the members of my race entertain no feelings of bitterness against the whites before and during the war, but there are many instances of Negroes tenderly caring for their former masters and mistresses who for some reason have become poor and dependent since the war. I know of instances where the former masters of slaves have for years been supplied with money by their former slaves to keep them from suffering. ... One sends him a little coffee or sugar, another a little meat, and so on. Nothing that the coloured people possess is too good for the son of 'old Mars' Tom,' who will perhaps never be permitted to suffer while any remain on the place who knew directly or indirectly of 'old Mars' Tom.'...

"From some things that I have said one may get the idea that some of the slaves did not want freedom. This is not true. I have never seen one who did not want to be free, or one who would return to slavery.

"I pity from the bottom of my heart any nation or body of people that is so unfortunate as to get entangled in the net of slavery. I have long since ceased to cherish any spirit of bitterness against the Southern white people on account of the enslavement of my race. No one section of our country was wholly responsible for its introduction, and, besides, it was recognized and protected for years by the General Government. Having once got its tentacles fastened on to the economic and social life of the Republic, it was no easy matter for the country to relieve itself of the institution. Then, when we rid ourselves of prejudice, or racial feeling, and look facts in the face, we must acknowledge that, notwithstanding the cruelty and moral wrong of slavery, the ten million Negroes inhabiting this country, who themselves or whose ancestors went through the school of American slavery, are in a stronger and more hopeful condition, materially, intellectually, morally, and religiously, than is true of an equal number of black people in any other portion of the globe. ...

"This I say, not to justify slavery — on the other hand, I condemn it as an institution, as we all know that in America it was established for selfish and financial reasons, and not from a missionary motive — but to call attention to a fact, and to show how Providence so often uses men and institutions to accomplish a purpose."

As for the future, Washington said: "When a Negro girl learns to cook, to wash dishes, to sew, to write a book, or a Negro boy learns to groom horses, or to grow sweet potatoes, or to produce butter, or to build a house, or to be able to practice medicine, as well or better than some one else, they will be rewarded regardless of race or colour. In the long run, the world is going to have the best, and any difference in race, religion, or previous history will not long keep the world from what it wants."

Nelson Mandela was beaten and imprisoned for almost three decades. When released at last, some supporters criticized him for showing too much grace and forgiveness toward his enemies. But Mandela's attitude toward forgiveness set the tone for the nation. After his death, a South African wrote:

"History now shows (Mandela) did lead South Africa back from the abyss. But he did more, and it was this that sealed his reputation forever. *He showed the world and his countrymen — black, white, rich, poor — that revenge is not the answer to years of injustice* (emphasis added). Who among us, in coming out of prison after 27 years, would have had the generosity to turn away from settling scores? Who among us would have refused to avenge ourselves on those who had treated us with such cruelty?

"But he did. Nelson Mandela sat down with his enemies and forgave them and moved on. And in doing so, he rescued his country, and he rescued each one of us, and gave us hope that there could be a future for our beautiful, fractured land. And for the greater earth that we all share."

Washington, born a slave, and Mandela, held captive for nearly 28 years, demonstrate the power of forgiveness — and of looking ahead. And these men forgave their actual oppressors.

My mother, born in the Jim Crow South, used to say, "The truth will not set you free — if delivered without hope." The "Hands Up, Don't Shoot" "movement" is neither truthful nor hopeful.

The Pontiff and 'Climate Change'

January 8, 2015

Move over, radical Islam. Step aside, poverty and political oppression. Pope Francis is expected to soon issue a rare papal encyclical, an official statement about what the pontiff believes is the world's most pressing issue — "climate change."

A month ago, during the U.N. climate change conference in Lima, Peru, the Pope warned of the dire consequences of climate change and declared that the "time to find global solutions is running out."

Last October, the Pope said: "An economic system centered on the god of money needs to plunder nature to sustain the frenetic rhythm of consumption that is inherent to it.

"'The system continues unchanged, since what dominates are the dynamics of an economy and a finance that are lacking in ethics. It is no longer man who commands, but money. Cash commands.

"'The monopolizing of lands, deforestation, the appropriation of water, inadequate agro-toxics are some of the evils that tear man from the land of his birth. Climate change, the loss of biodiversity and deforestation are already showing their devastating effects in the great cataclysms we witness."

So Pope Francis condemns both wealth "inequality" *and* greedy capitalism — at the same time. That is a contradiction.

History shows that raising a country's standard of living — addressing its wealth inequality — requires economic freedom and free markets, a.k.a. capitalism. Economist Milton Friedman said of all the economic systems known to man, capitalism, by far, moves more people out of poverty:

"The world runs on individuals pursuing their separate interests. The great achievements of civilization have not come from government bureaus. Einstein didn't construct his theory under order from a bureaucrat. Henry Ford didn't revolutionize the automobile industry that way. In the only cases in which the masses have escaped from the kind of grinding poverty you're talking about, the only cases in recorded history, are where they have had capitalism and largely free trade. If you want to know where the masses are worse off, worst off, it's exactly in the kinds of societies that depart from that. So that the record of history is absolutely crystal clear, that there is no alternative way, so far discovered, of improving the lot of the ordinary people that can hold a candle to the productive activities that are unleashed by the free-enterprise system."

The world's two most populous countries are China and India. In the last 50 years, both countries changed course and began pursuing free markets and encouraging entrepreneurship. As a result, tens of millions of people from India and China are no longer poor. The progress has been nothing short of staggering. Global inequality is declining — thanks to China and India, which account for more then one-third of the world's population. While the Chinese government avoids the "c" word — capitalism — its embrace of free-market reforms has lifted millions out of poverty. Similarly, in India freer markets spark a growth rate that now exceeds that of many countries in the West.

To repeat, worldwide income inequality is shrinking. The Atlantic magazine cites researchers who confirm the shrinking global inequality gap: "First, consider inequality. Academic researchers — from Xavier Sala-i-Martin of Columbia University, to Surjit Bhalla, formerly of the Brookings Institution and Rand Corporation, to Paolo Liberati of the University of Rome — all agree that global inequality is declining. That is because 2.6 billion people in China and India are richer than they used to be. Their economies are growing much faster than those of their Western counterparts, thus shrinking the income gap that opened at the dawn of industrialization in the 19th century, when the West took off and left much of the rest of the world behind.

"Paradoxically, the shrinking of the global inequality gap was only possible after India and China abandoned their attempts to create equality through central planning. By allowing people to keep more of the money they earned, the Chinese and Indian governments incentivized people to create more wealth. Allowing inequality to increase at home, in other words, diminished inequality globally. And global inequality, surely, is the statistic that should most concern the leader of a global religion."

Bono, the musician and philanthropist, has spent much of his life pursuing aid for Third World countries. But he had an epiphany. Capitalism, Bono said, lifts far more people out of poverty than aid ever will: "Aid is just a stop-gap. Commerce (and) entrepreneurial capitalism takes more people out of poverty than aid. ... In dealing with poverty here and around the world, welfare and foreign aid are a Band-Aid. Free enterprise is a cure. Entrepreneurship is the most sure way of development."

France's Other Problem — Job-Killing Economics

January 15, 2015

Islamic terrorists slaughtered 17 innocents in Paris in an attack described as "France's 9/11."

The two terrorist suspects at the satirical newspaper massacre are brothers, born and raised in France, children of parents who emigrated from Algeria. Some blame France's failure to "assimilate" Muslim youth on their attraction to violent jihad. While almost 25 percent of French youth is out of work, the number of young French Muslim people without jobs is over 40 percent. Muslims account for 10 percent of the French population but occupy 60 percent of its jails.

Never mind that Osama bin Laden was wealthy. Ayman al-Zawahiri, the current head of al-Qaida, is a doctor. Several of the terrorists who crashed planes into buildings and into Pennsylvania on 911 were middle-class or better, and several were college grads. But assuming "lack of opportunity" is a cause for the attraction to violent jihad, why does the French economy offer so few options? The answer is simple: job-killing economics.

At all levels of government, France takes over 44 percent of the earnings of its citizens. And this is before one assigns a cost to the numerous regulations placed on the shoulders of French entrepreneurs. In America, at all three levels — federal, state and local — government takes 33 percent of GDP, including mandates like Social Security. Add a cost to regulations mandated by state and local government, and UCLA economist Lee Ohanian says that government takes over 50 percent. Assume the same "cost percentage" that Americans pay for regulations to the French and you have a French economy where government takes about 65 percent of the earnings its people.

So what does France do? They elect a president, Francois Hollande, who literally said he "hates the rich." To demonstrate the hatred, the new president imposed a top marginal tax rate of 75 percent on incomes over 1 million euros. Rich people don't become rich for being stupid, so some did the commonsensical thing. Rich people left.

How idiotic are the economics in France? Get this. An employer, even one running a nonprofit, can hire a young worker and have the government pay up to 75 percent of his or her wages. Supposedly, this induces employers to hire young people. But from where does the money come? And how was it productive for government to subsidize salaries, let alone up to 75 percent!

About this scheme, the Wall Street Journal wrote: "By opening its wallet, the government is relying on the playbook of previous French presidents who financed jobs on a massive scale in an attempt to bend the unemployment curve. Those past measures, however, failed to change the overall trajectory of French unemployment and have left the country's job market larded with government-sponsored contracts. Companies took advantage of the incentives to snap up skilled workers, many of whom would probably have landed jobs without government subsidies. Employers also became accustomed to hiring young people at a discount."

In the Heritage Foundation's "2014 List of Economic Freedom," France continues its dismal performance: "France's economic freedom score is 63.5, making its economy the 70th freest in the 2014 Index. Its overall score has decreased by 0.7 point due to declines in monetary freedom, fiscal freedom, and business freedom. France is ranked 33rd out of 43 countries in the Europe region, and its overall score is slightly higher than the world average but below the regional average. Over the 20-year history of the Index, France's economic freedom has been stagnant, recording the fifth worst performance among advanced economies."

Urban pockets known as "les banlieues" surround many French cities. Some of these high-unemployment, high-crime ghettos have become literally off-limits for non-Muslims. Even police officers fear these areas where car-torching fires average 100 per night, according to an estimate by France's interior minister in 2013. Authorities estimate that 80 percent of France's car blazes are set out of anger and disaffection, while 20 percent are tied to insurance fraud.

The French population is aging. But its welfare state requires a constant infusion of younger workers to prop up the older retired ones. Trouble is many of the Muslim youth are, to say the least, disillusioned with France. According to a Pew Research poll conducted in 2006, 42 percent of young French Muslims believe suicide bombings are "often," "sometimes" or "rarely" "justified," with 35 percent of all French Muslims holding that view. Newsweek reported last year that a poll carried out by ICM for Russian news agency Rossiya Segodnya found 16 percent of all French citizens had a positive opinion of ISIS.

President Hollande's popularity has cratered along with the French economy. His poll numbers are now about 15 percent, and the idiotic 75 percent tax quietly expires at the end of this month. The bad news is that he has two years left on his term. Assuming, for the sake of argument, that the anger of French Muslim youth is tied to the dismal French economy, have you any fresh ideas, Mr. Hollande?

Selma Snub Vs. Eastwood Eclipse — Who's the Victim of Discrimination?

January 22, 2015

Where's the Clint Eastwood Million Cowboy March on Hollywood? The case for bias against Eastwood is far stronger than that of the alleged "snub" of the movie "Selma." "American Sniper," a new film directed by Clint Eastwood, set box-office records for a film opening in January. Yet he was "shut out" of the director category. Was Clint Eastwood, a white, unabashed George W. Bush-supporting Republican, a victim of political discrimination?

The Martin Luther King Jr. biopic received two Oscar nominations, one for "Best Picture." Cause for celebration? No, the Academy of Motion Picture Arts and Sciences "unexpectedly" overlooked the film's director and actors for the other prestigious categories.

For the second time since 1998, we are told, the academy named no "nominees of color" in the five important individual categories. We also learned that the 7,000 academy members, according to a 2013 Los Angeles Times report, are 93 percent white and 76 percent male. Obviously, racial insensitivity — if not racism.

Are these the same bigoted folk who last year awarded "12 Years A Slave" best picture, with best supporting actress going to Lupita Nyong'o? And what about the major Oscar nominations for films like "The Help" and other awards garnered by films like "The Butler"? And never mind that the current president of the Academy of Motion Picture Arts and Sciences is a black female.

Here's a "Selma Snub" sampling: "Why the Oscars' Omission of 'Selma' Matters" — The New York Times; "Oscars 2015:

Diversity is the Biggest Nomination Snub" — Los Angeles Times; "'Selma' Snubs Spur Twitter Backlash" — Chicago Tribune.

If Hollywood "snubs" black audiences' preferences, why do black households watch fare produced by Hollywood? A 2013 study by the TV marketing research firm Nielsen found blacks watch 37 percent more television than other demographics. "It's not only that the African-American audience watches more TV, but it's substantially more — two hours over other groups," said Ron Simon, head curator at The Paley Center for Media. And in 2013, according to the Motion Picture Association of America, blacks — while 12 percent of the population — accounted for 13 percent of movie ticket sales. Whites, at 63 percent of population, bought 54 percent of the movie tickets.

While we're at it, where's the Asian "outrage"?

There are, after all, few A-list Asian actors, and Asians have received fewer Oscar nominations than have blacks. Yet Indian, Filipino, Chinese and Japanese Americans have a higher median household income than Hispanic, black and white households. So much for the relationship between "seeing your own image on screen" and economic success.

A more serious controversy of "Selma" is its depiction of President Lyndon B. Johnson. In the film, he's falsely portrayed as an opponent of the Selma march and of the Voting Rights Act of 1965. He tries to get the FBI to discredit King. In reality, Johnson supported King, and J. Edgar Hoover's attempts to destroy King horrified Johnson. Julian Bond, a civil rights activist who worked with King and organized protests in Selma, says the movie got it wrong. Bond said, "I think the movie people wanted Dr. King to have an antagonist." This is not just creative license. It is a major departure from the truth.

But back to the "snub" of Selma vs. the "snub" of Eastwood.

Hollywood is blatantly anti-Republican, contemptuous of George W. Bush and hostile toward the Iraq War. Of Hollywood's political donations, 86 percent went to Democrats in 2008, and 79 percent in 2012. More than 90 percent of contributions by Hollywood celebrities to the 2012 presidential race went to Obama over Republican opponent Mitt Romney. DreamWorks' Jeffrey Katzenberg raised nearly $6.6 million for Obama's two presidential elections.

Many players don't even try to conceal their contempt.

Julia Roberts once said, "Republican comes in the dictionary just after 'reptile' and just above 'repugnant.'" For his book, "Primetime Propaganda: The True Hollywood Story of How the Left Took Over Your TV," conservative Ben Shapiro interviewed several Hollywood players. Many readily admitted conservatives are not welcome. They assumed, incorrectly, that Shapiro, a recent Harvard law grad, was one of them — a lefty who can barely conceal his contempt for the GOP. About television comedy shows, former ABC, CBS, and NBC top exec Fred Silverman said "there's only one perspective, and it's a very progressive perspective."

Shapiro said: "Everyone knows that people in Hollywood despise traditional conservatives. They think we're morons, bigots and Neanderthals. Over the course of doing research for this book, I spoke with hundreds of people in Hollywood. Few are conservative; even fewer are openly conservative. There's a reason for that — Hollywood insiders discriminate on a regular basis against conservatives. Many of them celebrate such discrimination. The same people who talk about tolerance and diversity have no tolerance for ideological diversity."

The Rev. Al Sharpton recently met with Sony co-studio head Amy Pascal over her alleged "racially insensitive" emails. Interestingly, after Sharpton's meeting, talk of Pascal losing her job seemed to die down.

NFL Tough Guys Need Dads, Too

January 29, 2015

"What do you think you missed not having a dad around?"

Marshawn Lynch, the grumpy, often-fined National Football League star for the defending Super Bowl champion Seattle Seahawks, was asked that question. Lynch, raised on the mean streets of Oakland, California, by a single mother, said: "Nothing. My mama played both parts."

When asked, however, why he finds it difficult to "trust" people, Lynch tells a story about his father: "I think it started earlier, when Mom would (take me over to my dad's) house. And when I get there, my dad like, 'Oh, OK, I be right back,' and then you don't see this guy for like, two days or something. And then after a while you, like, sh—, you build up numb feelings to that. So you start to expect the worst out of people."

Didn't he just tell us that he missed "nothing"?

Maurice Clarett, another inner-city football player who starred at Ohio State, was featured in an ESPN documentary film. Like Lynch, Clarett was raised without a father. "My father," explained Clarett, "wasn't part of my childhood. And when you come from a broken family you carry those problems; you carry that baggage wherever you go."

Clarett's mom added: "I provided all I could provide for him as a mother. There's just things a child pulls from a man. (Ohio State) coach (Jim) Tressel did represent a father figure to Maurice. They had conversations that a father and son should have. ... Tressel tried to provide some of the values that fathers instill. But Tressel can never be his father."

In Clarett's freshman year under coach Tressel, he played a key role in the Buckeye's winning the 2002 BCS National Championship. But Clarett's college career ended just months later, over accusations of academic misconduct and of filing a false police report. This resulted in an NCAA investigation and Clarett's suspension from Ohio State.

Alcohol- and drug-fueled days followed his Ohio State departure, and after three years, Clarett was arrested for armed robbery. His then-pregnant girlfriend feared that Clarett's unborn daughter would "grow up just like I did — with a father in prison."

Before his armed robbery trial began, Clarett was again arrested and ultimately convicted for illegal possession of loaded firearms and resisting arrest. Sentenced to seven-and-a-half years, he served three years and 11 months.

But instead of emerging from prison angry, Clarett says he "educated himself." His first lesson? Accepting responsibility for the choices he made that landed him in prison.

Some of his prison reflections:

"One thing that I've come to realize is I am my only enemy. I am the sole ruler of this journey."

"I hate to see my family suffer over my nonsense. They don't deserve it. My actions incarcerated them also."

"Quit searching for love, peace, and happiness outside of yourself. I once did that. It doesn't work."

"When I lockdown tonight I will begin to separate my emotions from my logic. That will bring clarity and sound judgment."

"When you're connected to positive people, when you're connected to people who uplift you, people who motivate you — that's how I come out of it. Show me your friends, I'll show you your future."

After his release from prison, Clarett's father died. He thought he was not going to have feelings. But he did. His father's death hurt him deeply, largely because, according to Clarett, he had a chance "to make it right with the man" — but chose not to do it.

Marshawn Lynch and Maurice Clarett are football "success" stories, backed by loving, self-sacrificing mothers. But for every talented inner-city athlete who "made it," there are many more with as much or more talent, with involved mothers, too — who never do.

It takes more than talent — it takes guidance to instill the necessary discipline to apply those skills.

President Barack Obama says: "We know the statistics — that children who grow up without a father are five times more likely to live in poverty and commit crime; nine times more likely to drop out of school and 20 times more likely to end up in prison."

My own father did not know his father. Raised in the Jim Crow South during the Great Depression, my father, like Maurice Clarett, vowed to be a better father than his non-existent one. In my latest book, "Dear Father Dear Son," I write about his tough life. After Pearl Harbor, he joined the Marines, where he became a staff sergeant in charge of food services. But after the war, when he returned to the South, he could not get work as a cook because restaurants told him, "We don't hire n—gers."

After working for years as a janitor, my dad opened up a restaurant, which he ran until his 80s. In "Dear Father," I write about my father and our 10-year estrangement when we didn't talk to each other. When at last we sat down for a lengthy — and long-overdue — conversation, I asked him about his father. And for the first time in my life, I saw my father cry.

Tough guys need dads, too.

Maybe the Rev can put in a word for Eastwood.

When Left-Wing Economists Gruber and Krugman Practiced Economics

February 5, 2015

President Barack Obama, in his State of the Union speech, called for a minimum-wage hike and for government-mandated paid family and medical leave.

"We are the only advanced country on Earth," said the President, "that doesn't guarantee paid sick leave or paid maternity leave to our workers." On the minimum wage, Obama issued this challenge: "And to everyone in this Congress who still refuses to raise the minimum wage, I say this: If you truly believe you could work full-time and support a family on less than $15,000 a year, try it. If not, vote to give millions of the hardest-working people in America a raise."

Minimum wage and paid family leave are not only moral imperatives, says Obama, but good economics to boot. Employees, he tells us, are happier and therefore more productive. Minimum wage and paid medical leave, understand, actually benefit business. It's just that dumb businessmen and women don't realize it.

But what does it say that perhaps the two most high-profile leftwing economists once opposed the minimum wage and paid family and medical leave?

When Obamacare architect/economist Jonathan Gruber and The New York Times economist Paul Krugman actually practiced economics, they both opposed the minimum wage. In Gruber's case, he also opposed government mandated for paid family and medical leave.

In 2011 — less than four years ago — Gruber gave an MIT lecture called "Applying Supply and Demand." About the minimum wage, Gruber said: "Let's say the government rolled in and set a minimum wage. ... Workers want to supply more hours than firms want to hire. ... You end up with excess supply. And we call that excess supply 'unemployment.'" He also insisted that a higher minimum wage pressures an employer to turn to automation: "We have a downward sloping demand curve, and why is it downward sloping? Because the higher the wage, the fewer workers the firm wants to hire. It would rather use machines instead."

As to paid leave, Gruber also argued against it. In 1994 Gruber wrote: "I study several state and federal mandates which stipulated that childbirth be covered comprehensively in health insurance plans, raising the relative cost of insuring women of childbearing age. I find substantial shifting of the costs of these mandates to the wages of the targeted group." In other words, Gruber said that an employer forced to pay for family leave will simply reduce the employee's wages to offset the cost — not net benefit to the employee.

This brings us to The New York Times columnist/economist Paul Krugman, who currently supports a $15 minimum wage. He, too, has done a 180 on the issue.

In 1998, Krugman reviewed a book that supported the living wage, titled "The Living Wage: Building a Fair Economy." But Krugman slammed the idea: "The living wage movement is simply a move to raise minimum wages through local action. So what are the effects of increasing minimum wages? Any Econ 101 student can tell you the answer: The higher wage reduces the quantity of labor demanded, and hence leads to unemployment."

Krugman even dismissed Card-Krueger, the widely cited minimum-wage study that purports to show its positive effect. Krugman pretty much dismissed it. "Indeed," he wrote, "much-cited studies by two well-regarded labor economists, David Card and Alan Krueger, find that where there have been more or less controlled experiments, for example when New Jersey raised minimum wages but Pennsylvania did not, the effects of the increase on employment have been negligible or even positive. Exactly what to make of this result is a source of great dispute. Card and Krueger offered some complex theoretical rationales, but most of their colleagues are unconvinced; the centrist view is probably that minimum wages 'do,' in fact, reduce employment, but that the effects are small and swamped by other forces. ...

"In short, what the living wage is really about is not living standards, or even economics, but morality. Its advocates are basically opposed to the idea that wages are a market price -? determined by supply and demand, the same as the price of apples or coal. And it is for that reason, rather than the practical details, that the broader political movement of which the demand for a living wage is the leading edge is ultimately doomed to failure: For the amorality of the market economy is part of its essence, and cannot be legislated away."

In sum, Gruber and Krugman once made Milton Friedman-like, Econ 101 arguments against minimum wage and its cousin, the livable wage. And in Gruber's case, he even argued against government-mandated paid family and medical leave.

The late Democratic Sen. Daniel Patrick Moynihan is attributed with the following quote: "You're entitled to your opinion, but you're not entitled to your own facts." In the case of Gruber and Krugman's current support for "progressive" policies they once opposed, what changed? The facts — or the politics?

Brian Williams: Selective Outrage and Double Standards

February 12, 2015

If Brian Williams, the anchor and face of NBC News, goes, others should march right out the door behind him.

Williams, in 2003, filed a report about his experiences in Iraq. He accurately reported that a helicopter an hour in front of his took fire from an RPG. But over the years the story morphed into Williams claiming that his helicopter took an incoming RPG and other small arms fire. Other stories Williams told and filed are under review, including apparently exaggerated or false claims filed or stated during Hurricane Katrina. Williams claimed he saw a dead body floating in the street outside his New Orleans hotel, and that his hotel had been assaulted by gangs. Neither of which apparently is true.

Due to concerns about the credibility of the $10-million-a-year newsreader, NBC announced Williams' six-month unpaid "suspension." Now six months is forever. When his replacement, the capable Lester Holt, settles in, soon it will likely be, "Brian, who?"

But what's the moral to the story — that we hold reporters to a high expectation of accuracy and journalistic integrity? Really? Williams works for the same company that gives an hour-long nightly platform to the Rev. Al Sharpton, America's preeminent race-card hustler.

As to Hurricane Katrina, reporters filed false story after story about murders, gunshots and rapes, many discredited — and many irresponsibly injecting the race issue. CNN's Wolf Blitzer, for example, said, "You simply get chills every time you see these poor individuals ... so tragically, so many of these people, almost all of them that we see, are so poor, and they are so black, and this is gonna raise lots of questions for people who are watching this story unfold." The ill treatment, Blitzer suggested, resulted from racism.

As for the importance of accuracy, CNN's Fareed Zakaria stands credibly accused of serial plagiarism. The left-of-center British publication The Week published a piece headlined, "Why Does Fareed Zakaria Still Have a Job?" Correspondent Ryan Cooper wrote: "CNN and Washington Post star Fareed Zakaria has committed dozens of acts of plagiarism and intellectual dishonesty. But Zakaria has not been hounded out of his job and shamed in the public square, as one would expect. Instead, he continues to go about his business as if nothing happened, revealing a disturbing double standard in the media industry."

Over at "60 Minutes," the married Steve Kroft reportedly bragged to his mistress that he enjoys a cozy relationship with President Barack Obama, whom Kroft calls "Barry." Conservatives have long accused Kroft of lobbing softball questions at Obama. Does Kroft's self-described status as Obama's "go-to" guy confirm conservatives' suspicion that he's in the tank for Obama? Crickets.

If exaggerations about war and war zones are career-ending for Brian Williams, does it apply to politicians?

Hillary Rodham Clinton, who could become our next president, falsely claimed that during a 1996 trip to Bosnia she took incoming fire. In 2008, she claimed: "I remember landing under sniper fire. There was supposed to be some kind of a greeting ceremony at the airport, but instead we just ran with our heads down to get into the vehicles to get to our base." But videotape showed no running, no head down, no snipers, no First-Lady-as-Rambo. And, as pre-arranged, she met a young Bosnian girl for the "greeting ceremony."

Sen. Tom Harkin, D-Iowa, served 30 years in the Senate, after 10 years in the House. From the book, "Stolen Valor," B.G. Burkett writes: "During a 1984 bid for reelection to the Senate ... Harkin boasted that he had served one year in Vietnam flying F-4s and F-8s on combat air patrols and photo-reconnaissance support missions. Challenged by Sen. Barry Goldwater, Harkin did a quick shuffle, claiming that he had actually flown combat sorties over Cuba during the sixties. Harkin finally admitted that he had not seen combat but had served as a ferry pilot stationed in Atsugi, Japan, flying aircraft to be repaired from Atsugi to the Philippines. When pressed by reporters to explain how much time he had really spent in Vietnam, Harkin estimated that over a year, he flew in and out of Vietnam a dozen or so times. But Harkin's military record showed no Vietnam service decorations. He finally conceded he had not flown combat air patrols in Vietnam and began describing himself as a Vietnam era vet."

What about Sen. Richard Blumenthal, D-Conn., who — many times — falsely claimed he served "in Vietnam" and that he faced hostility when he "returned"? In fact, he received five deferments after which, The New York Times reported, "He landed a coveted spot in the Marine Reserve, which virtually guaranteed that he would not be sent to Vietnam. He joined a unit in Washington that conducted drills and other exercises and focused on local projects, like fixing a campground and organizing a Toys for Tots drive." He now calls himself a "Vietnam-era vet."

But tales and puffery are unacceptable over at NBC. Not to worry, though. Brian Williams still has options. He can announce his candidacy for the 2016 presidential race — as a Democrat.

Hyper-Left Elizabeth Warren: Democrats' Fresh Face?

February 19, 2015

A shocking new poll shows Sen. Elizabeth Warren, D-Mass., ahead of Hillary Clinton in Iowa, the first caucus state, and in New Hampshire, the first primary state. The YouGov poll, paid for by Moveon.org, found Warren ahead of Clinton in Iowa, 31 percent to 24 percent, among likely Democratic primary and caucus voters. In New Hampshire, Warren's lead was 30 percent to 27 percent.

Other polls, however, show Clinton enjoying a substantial lead. This poll is an outlier, and the upstart 15-year-old polling firm gathers its data via the Internet, using complex methodology and algorithms. Some of their polls in recent years have been astonishingly accurate, even beating out the traditional big polling firms

YouGov pollsters conclude: "The results show that, after likely caucus goers and primary voters learn about Elizabeth Warren's biography and issue positions, not only do a stunning 79 percent say they want her to run, but, in both states, Warren ends up leading all other potential Democratic candidates in a head-to-head ballot question."

What's the appeal of Warren?

Her primary cause is her belief that investment firms and lending institutions need much more oversight. Specifically, Warren blames the Wall Street meltdown on the repeal of the Glass-Steagall Act, the Great Depression-era law that prevented commercial banks from engaging in traditional banking and vice versa. Glass-Steagall's repeal, argues Warren, is the primary reason for the Wall Street shenanigans she claims led to 2007-08's housing and stock market crashes.

In making this argument, Warren supports the majority conclusion of the Financial Crisis Inquiry Commission that Congress assembled to come up with the reasons for the crash. The commission consisted of six Democrats and four Republicans. The Democrats on the commission blamed Wall Street greed and traced the decline to a lack of regulations. But the Republicans took a very different view. They argued that the housing meltdown occurred after years of government-led policy that encouraged and pressured banks to lend to so-called "under represented" borrowers.

Three of the four Republicans wrote: "Fannie Mae and Freddie Mac did not by themselves cause the crisis, but they contributed significantly in a number of ways." The dissent of the fourth Republican also talked about impact of the Community Reinvestment Act and its 1995 revisions: "Although there were many contributing factors, the housing bubble of 1997-2007 would not have reached its dizzying heights or lasted as long, nor would the financial crisis of 2008 have ensued, but for the role played by the housing policies of the U.S. government over the course of two administrations." Nothing to do with the repeal of Glass-Steagall, and everything to do with bad government policies that encourage — and this Act really encourages — the irresponsible acquisition of real estate.

The repeal of Glass-Steagall did, indeed, allow for the existence of an organization like CitiGroup. But it was the investment firms like Bear Stearns and Lehman Brothers that led the crash. Again, Bear Stearns and Lehman Brothers were investment firms — that stayed in their lane.

By making the Glass-Steagall argument, Warren directly contradicts Bill Clinton, who still stands by his decision to sign the 1999 Gramm-Leach-Bliley Act, which repealed much of Glass-Steagall. The bill passed by 90 to 8 in the Senate and 362 to 57 in the House. In the unlikely event the president vetoed the bill, Congress had more than enough votes to override. But Clinton didn't veto it. He stands by his decision. The Hill, the publication that covers Congress, wrote a piece last year with this headline: "Bill Clinton Fires Back at Critics of His Financial Regulatory Policies": "Some progressives have blamed Clinton's 1999 repeal of Glass-Steagall, a

Depression-era law that separated investment and commercial banking, as one of the causes of the 2008 financial crisis. Clinton said that none of the financial institutions that failed during the financial crisis crashed because of Glass-Steagall's repeal. 'Not one.'"

A 2012 Forbes piece called, "Why the Glass-Steagall Myth Persists," supports Clinton's analysis: "By far, the single most cited example of this financial 'deregulation' is the Gramm-Leach-Bliley Act (GLBA), which partially repealed the Glass-Steagall Act 13 years ago today. Regulatory evangelists including Nobel Prize economist Joseph Stiglitz and recent senatorial candidate Elizabeth Warren, not to mention the Occupy Wall Street protesters, have named the overthrow of Glass-Steagall as public enemy number one.

"There is zero evidence GLBA unleashed the financial crisis. If you tally the institutions that ran into severe problems in 2008-09, the list includes Bear Stearns, Lehman Brothers, Merrill Lynch, AIG, and Fannie Mae and Freddie Mac, none of which would have come under Glass-Steagall's restrictions. Even President Obama has recently acknowledged that 'there is not evidence that having Glass-Steagall in place would somehow change the dynamic.'"

The hyperleft Warren is considered a "fresh face," which presumably refers to her comparatively shorter time in the public light. But she's just two years younger than Hillary Clinton. And just how far left — and unelectable — is the senator from Massachusetts? Warren makes Barack Obama look like Ronald Reagan.

Run, Warren, run!

Hollywood Hypocrites Demand 'Wage Equality'

February 26, 2015

When actress Patricia Arquette won an Oscar, she pled for "wage equality" for women: "To every woman who gave birth to every taxpayer and citizen in this nation: We have fought for everybody else's equal rights. It's our time to have wage equality once and for all and equal rights for women in the United States of America."

Days later, presumptive Democratic presidential nominee Hillary Clinton said, "I think we all cheered at Patricia Arquette's speech at the Oscars, because she's right — it's time to have wage equality." Back in April 2014, Hillary Clinton sent out this tweet: "20 years ago, women made 72 cents on the dollar to men. Today it's still just 77 cents. More work to do."

Today women, supposedly, only make 77 cents on the dollar for doing the same work as men. Here's the problem — it simply is not true. When you compare apples to apples, the earnings gap shrinks to between four and seven cents, and the Labor Department suggests "non-sexist" reasons explain even this small gap.

The Department of Labor commissioned a study from an organization called CONSAD Research Corporation. The report, which came out in 2009, is called "An Analysis of Reasons for the Disparity in Wages Between Men and Women." In its foreword, The Labor Department concedes that the "gap" is a myth:

"There are observable differences in the attributes of men and women that account for most of the wage gap. Statistical analysis that includes those variables has produced results that collectively account for between 65.1 and 76.4 percent of a raw gender wage gap of 20.4 percent, and thereby leave an adjusted gender wage gap that is between 4.8 and 7.1 percent."

The Labor Department also said that the remaining gap could be explained by choices that men and women make. Specifically:

"A greater percentage of women than men tend to work part-time. Part-time work tends to pay less than full-time work.

"A greater percentage of women than men tend to leave the labor force for childbirth, child care and elder care. Some of the wage gap is explained by the percentage of women who were not in the labor force during previous years, the age of women, and the number of children in the home.

"Women, especially working mothers, tend to value 'family friendly' workplace policies more than men."

This brings us back to Hillary Clinton. Does she practice "wage equality"?

An analysis by the Washington Free Beacon found Clinton paid the women on her Senate staff 72 cents for each dollar she paid the men:

"During (2002 to 2008), the median annual salary for a woman working in Clinton's office was $15,708.38 less than the median salary for a man, according to the analysis of data compiled from official Senate expenditure reports."

President Barack Obama's White House female staffers also earn less than the male staffers. According to the 2011 annual report on White House staff, female White House employees earn a median annual salary of $60,000 — or 18 percent less than male employees' $71,000 salary. Last July, an analysis by The Washington Post found "the White House has not narrowed the gap between the average pay of male and female employees since President Obama's first year in office."

In 2012, after several female senators called a press conference to push for gender "paycheck fairness," the Washington Free Beacon looked at the salary "equality" in the their own offices:

"(Patty) Murray, (D-Wash.), who has repeatedly accused Republicans of waging a 'war on women,' is one of the worst offenders. Female members of Murray's staff made about $21,000 less per year than male staffers in 2011, a difference of 33.8 percent. ... A significant 'gender gap' exists in (Dianne) Feinstein's (D-

Calif.) office, where women also made about $21,000 less than men in 2011, but the percentage difference — 41 percent — was even higher than Murray's. (Barbara) Boxer's (D-Calif.) female staffers made about $5,000 less, a difference of 7.3 percent."

Arquette's plea comes after the Sony Pictures cyber attack. Publically disclosed private emails shows that then co-studio chief Amy Pascal paid Jennifer Lawrence less money than her not-as-popular male co-stars in "American Hustle" — and this was after Lawrence starred in the blockbuster "Hunger Games."

When asked why, Ms. Pascal was blunt: "Here's the problem: I run a business. People want to work for less money, I'll pay them less money. I don't call them up and say, 'Can I give you some more?' Because that's not what you do when you run a business. The truth is, what women have to do is not work for less money. They have to walk away. People shouldn't be so grateful for jobs. ... People should know what they're worth." Pascal, like Patricial Arquette, is also a contributor to the "pay equity" Democratic Party.

For his second term, President Obama wants to combat "income inequality." To get started, he won't even have to leave the White House.

Ethanol: The GOP-Supported Rip-Off

March 5, 2015

Can someone explain why the "party of limited government" continues, with a straight face, to support ethanol? Republican Sen. Chuck Grassley of Iowa says about the heavily subsided product, "Everything about ethanol is good, good, good."

Really? Really? Really?

Supporters of ethanol — which we make from corn — say it reduces our dependence on foreign oil, is cheaper and aids the environment because it burns cleaner than non-blended fossil fuels. In 1996, The New York Times wrote: "At a time when Congress has been overhauling the nation's systems of agricultural subsidies, and public officials across the country have considered huge cuts in benefits to big corporations, ethanol has been untouched. Largely through the efforts of (then soon-to-be 1996 GOP presidential nominee Sen. Bob Dole of Kansas), it has remained one of the most subsidized American industries."

Dole's office said, "As a national leader on agriculture policy, Sen. Dole is a longtime supporter of this clean-burning all-American renewable fuel to promote new markets for American grain, jobs for our nation's farm belt and energy self-sufficiency." The statement noted that Kansas contained 13,500 corn farms and four ethanol plants.

That was nearly 20 years ago. The rip-off continues.

The New York Times recently wrote about the wooing of deep-pocket Republican donors by the 2016 presidential hopefuls: "Some of the gatherings are expressly intended to bring candidates in line with the policy positions of donors on issues like government spending and foreign policy. While Mr. (Bruce) Rastetter's agriculture forum will cover a range of issues, much of the advocacy surrounding the event, including a 'V.I.P. press reception' featuring Iowa's Republican governor, is aimed at pushing the candidates to support the Renewable Fuel Standard, which is coveted by the ethanol industry."

Who is Rastetter? He's a "prominent 'super PAC' donor" who organized the Iowa Agriculture Summit where, per the Times: "Each (Republican presidential hopeful) will submit questions from Mr. Rastetter ... whose business interests range from meat processing to ethanol production."

How do the facts line up with the wondrous claims about ethanol — clean burning, cheap and decreases our dependency on foreign sources?

Ethanol increases the demand for corn, which means corn prices go up. This causes prices for farmland to rise. It also raises the prices for animal feed, which makes food prices go up. Not just on meat — prices have gone up on poultry and dairy products, as well as foodstuffs containing cornstarch, cornmeal, corn syrup and other corn products. Meanwhile, the U.S., which as recently as 2007 supplied two-thirds of the world's corn with its exports, now supplies only a little over one-third. And the amount of corn used to produce the ethanol to fill one SUV's gas tank could feed one person for one year.

Today, according to the USDA, ethanol accounts for roughly 6.6 percent of total transport fuel consumption, but consumes about 40 percent of the U.S. corn supply.

In 2007, Rolling Stone's Jeff Goodell wrote in "The Ethanol Scam": "Ethanol doesn't burn cleaner than gasoline, nor is it cheaper. Our current ethanol production represents only 3.5 percent of our gasoline consumption — yet it consumes twenty percent of the entire U.S. corn crop, causing the price of corn to double in the last two years and raising the threat of hunger in the Third World. And the increasing acreage devoted to corn for ethanol means less land for other staple crops, giving farmers in South America an incentive to carve fields out of tropical forests that help to cool the planet and stave off global warming."

The ethanol-increased demand for corn also entices more farmers to plant more land with corn, instead of balancing their risk by planting other crops. Goodell wrote: "Corn is already the most subsidized crop in America, raking in a total of $51 billion in federal handouts between 1995 and 2005 — twice as much as wheat subsidies and four times as much as soybeans. Ethanol itself is propped up by hefty subsidies, including a fifty-one-cent-per-gallon tax allowance for refiners. And a study by the International Institute for Sustainable Development found that ethanol subsidies amount to as much as $1.38 per gallon — about half of ethanol's wholesale market price."

What about the environment?

Goodell writes: "But as a gasoline substitute, ethanol has big problems: Its energy density is one-third less than gasoline, which means you have to burn more of it to get the same amount of power. It also has a nasty tendency to absorb water, so it can't be transported in existing pipelines and must be distributed by truck or rail, which is tremendously inefficient."

Ethanol is a rip-off, pure and simple. Aside from fattening the coffers of ethanol producers like Archer Daniels Midland, it is not justifiable on any basis, not least from a Republican Party that supposedly believes in free, unfettered, non-subsidized markets. Ethanol is an inexcusable theft from taxpayers. That the Republican leadership still supports this undermines the "Republican message" and makes the party look like a band of hypocrites.

The Farcical Ferguson Report

March 12, 2015

The NBA consists of 76 percent black players. But blacks are just 13 percent of the country. Clearly, the league engages in racial discrimination against whites. Silly, right? Well, this is exactly what the sleight-of-hand Department of Justice pulled off to find that the Ferguson Police Department engages in "implicit and explicit racial bias"!

The report insults anybody who's ever studied the statistics ?- or logic.

The 105-page report concludes: "Ferguson's law enforcement practices are shaped by the City's focus on revenue rather than by public safety needs. This emphasis on revenue has compromised the institutional character of Ferguson's police department, contributing to a pattern of unconstitutional policing, and has also shaped its municipal court, leading to procedures that raise due process concerns and inflict unnecessary harm on members of the Ferguson community. Further, Ferguson's police and municipal court practices both reflect and exacerbate existing racial bias, including racial stereotypes. Ferguson's own data establish clear racial disparities that adversely impact African Americans. The evidence shows that discriminatory intent is part of the reason for these disparities. Over time, Ferguson's police and municipal court practices have sown deep mistrust between parts of the community and the police department, undermining law enforcement legitimacy among African Americans in particular."

The Washington Post immediately put out an article headlined "The 12 key highlights from the DOJ's scathing Ferguson report." Per the Post, the "scathing" statistic first listed is this: Ferguson is 67 percent black, but blacks comprised 85 percent of the traffic stops and 93 percent of the arrests. Incontrovertible proof that the Ferguson PD engages in institutional racism!

Reporters, in describing the Ferguson report, used adjectives that include "shocking," "stunning" and "eye-popping."

But if Ferguson's numbers are "eye-popping," what adjective applies to the New York City Police Department. New York City is 25 percent black. However, of the traffic stops, blacks comprise 55 percent. The statistical "gap" is 30 points. In Ferguson, as stated, the black population is 67 percent, but 85 percent of the traffic stops. The statistical "gap" is 18 points — far smaller than New York's 30-point "gap."

Why aren't Messrs. Al Sharpton, Jesse Jackson and Eric Holder marching on Times Square?

The answer is that the liberal former New York City Mayor Michael Bloomberg, who governed for 12 years, defends the aggressive policing of the NYPD — and the resulting "statistical disparities." Bloomberg says: "Unlike many cities, where wealthy areas get special treatment, the NYPD targets its manpower to the areas that suffer the highest crime levels. Ninety percent of all people killed in our city — and 90 percent of all those who commit the murders and other violent crimes — are black and Hispanic. It is shameful that so many elected officials and editorial writers have been largely silent on these facts.

"Instead, they have argued that police stops are discriminatory because they do not reflect the city's overall census numbers. By that flawed logic, our police officers would stop women as often as men and senior citizens as often as young people. To do so would be a colossal misdirection of resources and would take the core elements of police work — targeting high-crime neighborhoods and identifying suspects based on evidence — out of crime-fighting. ...

"That the proportion of stops generally reflects our crime numbers does not mean ... that the police are engaged in racial profiling; it means they are stopping people in those communities who fit descriptions of suspects or are engaged in suspicious activity."

The National Institute of Justice is the research and evaluation agency of the DOJ. In 2013, the NIJ published its study called "Race, Trust and Police Legitimacy." Unlike when responding to dispatch calls, police officers exercise more discretion when it comes to traffic stops. Thus, the supposedly "racial profiling" cops can have a field day when it comes to traffic stops, right?

But according to the NIJ, 3 out of 4 black drivers admit being stopped by police for a "legitimate reason." Blacks, compared to whites, were on average more likely to commit speeding or other traffic offenses. "Seatbelt usage," said the NIJ, "is chronically lower among black drivers. If a law enforcement agency aggressively enforces seatbelt violations, police will stop more black drivers." The NIJ conclusion? Numerical disparities result from "differences in offending" in addition to "differences in exposure to the police" and "differences in driving patterns."

President Obama, backed by research from the left and from the right, said, "Children who grow up without a father are five times more likely to live in poverty and commit crime; nine times more likely to drop out of school and 20 times more likely to end up in prison."

Richmond, Virginia, is a city of 214,000, with a black population of 50 percent. Eighty-six percent of black Richmond families are headed by a single parent. Of Ferguson's 67 percent black population, how many kids grew up in fatherless homes?

Whatever the answer, isn't this a far more relevant statistic?

Gen. Powell, Who Are the GOP's 'Dark Veins'?

March 19, 2015

The Republican Party, says former Secretary of State Gen. Colin Powell, suffers from a "dark vein of intolerance." We salute Powell's service. He is a heavily decorated vet who served two tours of duty in Vietnam when things were hot and heavy over there.

But General, care to name names? Who are these "intolerant" Republicans? Why engage in accusation by innuendo? By all means, name them, shame them — make them famous.

In the meantime, while Powell composes his list, we compile some questions to some possible left-leaning "dark veins of intolerance":

What color was Rep. Maxine Waters', D-Calif., "vein" when she said, "The tea party can go straight to hell"?

What color was Tavis Smiley's "vein" when he said former President Ronald Reagan "tortured" blacks?

What color was Spike Lee's "vein" when he said, "I'm convinced AIDS is a government-engineered disease"?

What color was Rep. Charlie Rangel's, D-N.Y., "vein" when he said, "George W. Bush is our Bull Connor"?

What color was Harry Belafonte's "vein" when asked whether the number and prominence of blacks in the Bush administration suggested a lack of racism, said, "Hitler had a lot of Jews high up in the hierarchy of the Third Reich"?

What color was Danny Glover's "vein" when he called America "one of the main purveyors of violence in this world"?

What color was Bill Cosby's "vein" when he said AIDS "was started by human beings to get after certain people they don't like"?

What color was Will Smith's "vein" when he said, "AIDS was created as a result of biological-warfare testing"?

What color was Harry Belafonte's "vein" when he said, "We are living in terrorism as black people in America. And it has been that way since the dawning of slavery"?

What color was then-NAACP chairman Julian Bond's "vein" when he said, "The Republican Party would have the American flag and the swastika flying side by side."

What color was the vein of ex-U.N. ambassador Andrew Young, a man who marched with Martin Luther King, when he criticized convenience store operators in the inner city: "First it was Jews, then it was Koreans and now it's Arabs" who have "ripped off" blacks?

What color was feminist attorney Gloria Allred's "vein" when she referred to you and then-national security advisor Condoleezza Rice as "Uncle Tom types"?

What was the color of the Congressional Black Caucus's "vein" when they denied white Rep. Steve Cohen, D-Tenn., admission to the caucus — though his district is 60 percent black? In denying him admission, one CBC member — the son of the caucus's co-founder — said of their blacks-only membership, "It's an unwritten rule."

What color was Al Sharpton's "vein" when he called black New York City then-Mayor David Dinkins a "n—ger whore"?

What color was NAACP Julian Bond's "vein" when he said then-President George W. "Bush selected nominees from the Taliban wing of American politics ... and chose Cabinet officials whose devotion to the Confederacy is nearly canine in its uncritical affection."

What color was Sen. (then-candidate) Claire McCaskill's, D-Mo., "vein" when, after Hurricane Katrina, she said President Bush "let people die on rooftops in New Orleans because they were poor and because they were black."

What color was Jesse Jackson's "vein" when he called Jews "Hymies" and New York City "Hymie-town"?

What color was Bill Clinton's "vein" when, according to the book "Game Change," he said about Obama, "A few years ago, this guy would have been getting us coffee"?

What color was Harry Reid's "vein" when he said about then-presidential candidate Obama, he's "light-skinned" with "no Negro dialect" unless he wants one?

What color was lefty Spike Lee's "vein" when he said he disliked "interracial couples" — and gives them visual "daggers"?

What color was lefty Rep. Diane Watson's, D-Calif., "vein" when she slammed a black opponent for marrying a white woman: "He's married to a white woman. He wants to be white. He wants a colorless society. He has no ethnic pride. He doesn't want to be black."

What color was Rep. Waters' "vein" when she called then-President George Herbert Walker Bush "a racist"?

What color was Charlie Rangel's "vein" when he said about the GOP, "It's not 'sp-c' or 'n—ger' anymore. They say 'let's cut taxes'"?

Finally, General, every year Ebony magazine publishes its "Power 100," the list of "most influential" black Americans. Every year, the magazine excludes prominent black conservatives including Supreme Court Justice Clarence Thomas. It shuts out Walter Williams, one the nation's most popular syndicated columnists, author of several books on economics and race, and former economics department chairman of George Mason University.

Ebony also excludes the man playwright David Mamet calls, "our greatest contemporary philosopher." Economist Thomas Sowell's weekly column appears in hundreds of newspapers. His books on economics, culture and race are absolute reads for those who study why some races, cultures and ethnicities survive while others perish.

These are just some of those on the left who possess "dark veins." Gen. Powell, your turn.

Four (Black) Cops Killed in Seven Days — Where's the Outrage?

March 26, 2015

Wednesday, March 4: Fulton County police detective Terence Avery Green was killed, shot in the head by a suspect. According to WXIA-TV, Atlanta: "Police responded to a shots fired call early Wednesday. They were told the suspect was possibly intoxicated. Neighbors said the man was going from house to house, banging on doors and firing a long barrel gun. ...

"(Fulton County Assistant Police Chief Gary) described the situation as an ambush, saying the officers 'were trying to do their job, they were trying to protect this neighborhood from someone who was shooting. And they had no other option but to do their job. And the way it appears to me, they were ambushed without warning.' ...

"Green was a veteran officer with nearly 22 years of service. He is survived by his parents and his four sons."

Thursday, March 5: Officer Robert Wilson III, while on duty and in uniform, walked into a game store to purchase a gift for his son. Two men robbed the store, and shot and killed Officer Wilson. According to CNN: "Wilson was standing at the counter across from employees at the GameStop store when two brothers, Carlton Hipps and Ramone Williams, walked in carrying guns, police said.

"They allegedly stuck up the store with at least five patrons and two employees inside.

"'They said they thought it was going to be an easy target,' said police spokesman Capt. James Clark. ... Wilson confronted (the suspects), and a firefight broke out, police said.

"The officer, an eight-year veteran, stepped away from others in the store to keep them out of the crossfire, police said after watching the store's security camera footage.

"He was a hero and a warrior, Clark said. "He fought until the very, very end, firing at both of them."... Within 30 to 40 seconds, 50 shots fell, he said. ...

"Wilson was 30 years old. In addition to his son, he leaves behind a 1-year-old daughter. His son turns 10 on Monday. The game was also going to be a birthday present."

Saturday, March 7: Police Officer Brennan Rabain was killed while trying to make a traffic stop on a speeding driver. The officer lost control of his squad car and crashed into a fence. According to the local NBC affiliate news: "Police are searching for anyone who may have witnessed a crash that killed a Prince George's County police officer. ... Rabain had been off duty, but when he initiated the traffic stop, he went back on duty, police said." Rabain, 27, had been with the department less than two years, and leaves behind a 3-year-old daughter.

Tuesday, March 10: Deputy U.S. Marshal Josie Wells, 27, was killed in a shootout near Baton Rouge, Louisiana, as he attempted to apprehend a fugitive accused of killing a brother and sister.

According the Associated Press: "The fugitive, Jamie D. Croom, 31, was shot and taken to a hospital. ... Croom was wanted in the shooting deaths of a brother and sister in New Roads, Louisiana. ...

"The shootout took place in Scotlandville, an area north of Baton Rouge. A task force made by federal Marshals was serving an arrest warrant when the shootout happened. ... Croom, a resident of New Roads, had a lengthy criminal record, (local Sheriff Beauregard) Torres said. 'He was a dangerous criminal,' Torres said. 'It was a very high price to pay for this warrant to bring this man into custody. It was a very, very high price.'

"Wells was a graduate of East Central High School in Hurley, Mississippi, and of Jackson State University. 'He was a tremendous student,' East Central Principal James Hughey told WLOX-TV. 'He was very well liked.' ... Wells' father, Obie Wells Sr., is a retired Jackson County sheriff's deputy. His brother, Obie Wells Jr., is an officer with the Jackson Police Department in the state capital.

"'His dad was so proud of him for being a U.S. marshal,' (Mississippi state Rep. Manly) Barton said." The day after his death, Wells' wife — who is pregnant with the couple's first child — learned the sex of their baby. She is having a boy, and she plans to name him Josie Wells, Jr.

Last year, according to the nonprofit National Law Enforcement Officers Memorial Fund, 126 federal, state, local, tribal and territorial officers died in the line of duty in 2014 — although some deaths were attributed to health problems or traffic accidents. Fifty officers were killed by firearms, 15 of them in ambush attacks.

The memorial fund says that shootings against officers increased 50 percent in 2014. This total includes two NYPD officers killed in December in an ambush. The suspect, killed by police, had posted Internet messages that accused police of racism, threatened to kill officers and urged others to do the same.

Despite the widely publicized recent cases where cops killed blacks, new studies show cops — black and white — more reluctant to shoot a black suspect compared to a white suspect. Reasons are unclear, but fear of additional scrutiny — whether fair or not — might be a factor.

Suspects who kill cops, however, appear colorblind.

Sen. Dick Durbin and the Race Card

April 2, 2015

Does Sen. Dick Durbin, D-Ill., suffer from short, medium and long-term memory loss?

In criticizing Republicans for holding up the nomination of Loretta Lynch, Durbin said, "Loretta Lynch, the first African-American woman nominated to be attorney general, is asked to sit in the back of the bus when it comes to the Senate calendar." Race card alert!

Does Durbin not recall voting against Miguel Estrada and even participating in a filibuster against the man who would have been the first Hispanic on the U.S. Court of Appeals for the D.C. Circuit?

Estrada was born in Honduras. He immigrated to the United States when he was 17, arriving with a limited command of English. He graduated magna cum laude and Phi Beta Kappa with a bachelor's degree from Columbia in 1983. He graduated magna cum laude in 1986 from Harvard Law School, where he became editor of the Harvard Law Review. After law school, Estrada served as a law clerk to Judge Amalya L. Kearse of the U.S. Court of Appeals for the Second Circuit. He then clerked for Justice Anthony M. Kennedy of the U.S. Supreme Court for two years.

From 1990 until 1992, Estrada served as assistant U.S. attorney and deputy chief of the Appellate Section, U.S. Attorney's Office, Southern District of New York. In 1992, he joined the United States Department of Justice as an assistant to the solicitor general for the George H. W. Bush administration, where he served with now-Chief Justice John G. Roberts. He has argued 22 cases before the United States Supreme Court.

But Estrada, after two years of waiting, finally withdrew his nomination for the Court of Appeals.

Does Durbin not recall voting against Alberto Gonzales, the first Hispanic U.S. attorney general?

Alberto Gonzales was born to a Catholic family in San Antonio, Texas, and raised in Houston. Of Mexican descent, he was one of eight children born to his stay-at-home mother and construction-worker father, who met each other when both were migrant workers. Gonzales and his family of 10 lived in a two-bedroom house with no running hot water and — until Gonzales was in high school — no phone, either.

A high school honor student, Gonzales enlisted and served in the U.S. Air Force after graduation. He received an appointment to the U.S. Air Force Academy, and later transferred to Rice University in Houston, where he earned a bachelor's degree with honors in political science in 1979. He got his law degree from Harvard in 1982, and began practicing law at a prestigious firm in Houston.

Does Durbin not recall voting against Janice Rogers Brown, the second black female on the U.S. Court of Appeals for the D.C. Circuit?

Born in Greenville, Alabama, Brown, a sharecropper's daughter, attended majority black schools as a child. Her family refused to enter businesses that segregated blacks. She earned her B.A. from California State University Sacramento in 1974 and her law degree from the UCLA School of Law in 1977.

Finally, does Durbin not recall voting against the confirmation of Condoleezza Rice, the first black female secretary of state?

Rice was born in Birmingham, Alabama, the only child of a schoolteacher/church organist and a football coach/Presbyterian minister. She grew up in the then-deeply segregated Jim Crow South. Rice knew two of the four little black girls killed while attending Sunday school during the tragic 1963 firebombing at Birmingham's Sixteenth Street Baptist Church.

Rice began piano lessons at the age of three. She studied French and Spanish, and became a competitive figure skater. Attending segregated schools, Rice excelled, skipping the first and seventh grades. She attended an integrated public school for the first time in the 10th grade, when her family moved to Denver, Colorado. She finished her last year of high school and her first year at the University of Denver at the same time, at the age of 15.

She earned her bachelor's degree in political science from the University of Denver in 1974; her master's from the University of Notre Dame in 1975; and her Ph.D. from the University of Denver's Graduate School of International Studies in 1981. That same year, she joined Stanford University as a political science professor. In 1993, Rice became the first woman and first African-American to serve as provost of Stanford University — a post she held for six years.

To lefties like Durbin, a metamorphosis occurs to conservative women and people of color. Gloria Steinem, for example, once called Republican Sen. Kay Bailey Hutchison a "female impersonator." Conservative blacks cease being black. They're sellouts. Conservative Latinos are no longer Latino. They're "Tio Tacos." They are, you see, conservatives, a form of political subspecies. They are ideological doormats that Democrats can enthusiastically attack, and then — with a straight face — call Republicans "racist."

Astonishing.

Obama's Iran Deal: Someday the World Will Cry, 'Why?!'

April 9, 2015

Barack Obama is a young man. By the time he leaves office, he will be in his mid-50s. Based on life expectancy, he could live for another 40 years or so. So he will be around to see the full consequences of his disastrous Iran nuclear "framework."

The deal is done.

No matter what Republicans do, Europeans fully intend to let sanctions expire. They just needed an excuse to do so, an excuse that Obama provided. Someday, nations will ask why the world's superpower ignored chants of "death to America" and "death to Israel" and allowed Iran to slow-walk toward getting nuclear weapons.

A little recent history. Under the watchful eye of the International Atomic Energy Agency, North Korea became a nuclear power — despite having signed a nuclear non-proliferation treaty. For 25 years, as it developed its nuclear bomb, North Korea insisted it had no such plans. Then-President Clinton dispatched former President Jimmy Carter to dissuade the North Koreans. Carter was convinced of North Korea's sincerity. Carter said: "The world in 1994 was marching toward a war that was neither wanted nor necessary. ... I hoped that Kim Il-Sung was looking for a way to resolve the crisis peacefully. ... My expectations proved to be correct. Kim Il-Sung wanted to deal, and he and I negotiated an agreement."

Carter triumphantly announced on CNN the terms of the deal he brokered to get North Korea, he said, that got them to end their nuclear program. North Korea took the economic assistance — and continued its nuclear program. Shortly after Carter's visit, North Korea became an acknowledged nuclear power. These "successful" talks led, in part, to Carter's receiving the Nobel Peace Prize in 2002. Unfortunately, days after the announcement of Carter's Peace Prize, North Korea publicly admitted that it never ended its nuclear program — and that the country intended to continue it.

Obama, as a candidate, called a nuclear-armed Iran "unacceptable." Well, was anyone listening when National Intelligence Director James Clapper said Iran could make nuclear weapons "right now"? "It's a political decision for them," Clapper said to PBS's Charlie Rose, "not that they don't have the technical wherewithal, the technical competence, because they do." Clapper said Iran's supreme leader simply has not made the "political decision" to make the weapon!

Immediately after the announced framework, Iran disputed the White House's characterization on major issues. No, said Iran, the sanctions are to be lifted right away. No, said Iran, we are not rolling back any of our nuclear facilities. And no, said Iran, we have not consented to "no notice" inspections, the *only* way to give real assurance that Iran won't cheat as easily as it has already.

Military experts say it's too late for Israel to take military action. Iran is now too far gone, too prepared, having dispersed sleeper cells to strike on cue. At least one of Iran's nuclear facilities is underground and difficult to bomb. Why the need for an underground facility if it is for "peaceful purposes"?

The world will someday ask how a nation that funded and founded the terror group Hezbollah could be allowed to get a bomb. The leader of Hezbollah stated that he hopes all the Jews do return to Israel — that way they can be eliminated in one fell swoop. So much for the notion that the problem in the Middle East is Israel. Hezbollah leader Hassan Nasrallah wants to hunt down and kill Jews outside of Israel.

Days after last week's "historic" nuclear deal, CBS reported that in Iranian mosques, worshipers *still* chanted "death to America." But, CBS hopefully tells us, they're doing this out of "more habit than conviction." Iran has lied from the beginning, has always lied and is lying now. If, after all, this deal is about inspiring confidence, why wasn't the recognition of Israel — as a Jewish state — a nonnegotiable part of the deal? But Obama dismissed it out of hand: "The notion ... (of) Iran recognizing Israel ... is, I think, a fundamental misjudgment."

Finally, what makes Obama and the Democrats believe that ISIS, al-Qaida and the assorted related groups have only regional aspirations? The goal of jihad, as stated by the current head of al-Qaida, is to eventually ignite a battle between the West and the Muslim world. And, at the climactic moment, Allah is expected to appear and shift the balance of victory to the Muslim warriors.

Sound crazy? Insane? This is exactly why such people should never acquire nuclear weapons. Obama will someday have to answer the question, "How could you allow that to happen?"

I hope and pray that I am wrong.

Chicago: Economic Death Spiral After 84 Years of Democratic Control

April 16, 2015

Chicago Mayor Rahm Emanuel, after winning reelection, pronounced Chicago "the greatest city in America." Run by Democrats for more than eight decades, Chicago should serve as a showplace that reflects the wonderful world of "progressive policies."

Public schools are a mess, and the city's finances place their bonds at near junk level. In 2013, the city averaged 36 homicides a month, with the majority of them unsolved.

CNN aired a series on Chicago called "Chicagoland," starring the city's dynamic mayor. Presumably, Emanuel thought it would show off the mayor as he tackled the city's problems. Why, if the man his own mom calls "Rahmbo" can lead Chicago as a prosperous, well-run city, imagine the job he'd do as president of the United States. But the idea backfired — and not because Emanuel isn't dynamic or hard-working.

The eight-part series showed a beleaguered city, struggling to get by on limited funds. In one episode, a valiant but embattled inner-city high school principal literally maps out "safe passage zones" — routes her students could take to and from school to avoid gang violence. Think of it. A public school principal literally advising students on how they can go to and from school — without getting shot.

Welcome to Chicagoland.

A recent piece in the National Journal pronounced Chicago a "broken city:" "Perhaps more than any other major city in America,

Chicago is facing a truly grave set of problems — problems that are essentially more extreme versions of the challenges confronting city governments across the country.

"The quandaries begin with Chicago's dramatic social divide. To an even greater extent than is the case in, say, New York or Philadelphia, Chicago has become two entirely separate cities. One is a bustling metropolis that includes the Loop, Michigan Avenue's Magnificent Mile, and the Gold Coast, as well as the city's well-to-do, working-class, and upwardly mobile immigrant neighborhoods. The other Chicago consists of impoverished neighborhoods on the far South and West Sides, primarily populated by African-Americans. These places have remained beyond the reach of the city's recovery from the Great Recession.

"Meanwhile, even as it grapples with this extreme gap, Chicago is suffering from a severe fiscal crisis. Like plenty of other municipalities, Chicago lacks the revenue to pay its bills, particularly its pension obligations to city workers. According to a 2013 Pew report, 61 other U.S. cities face similar difficulties, but Chicago's situation is one of the worst. ... If the gaping holes in Chicago's social and fiscal fabric ... can't be fixed ... (t)hen Chicago may end up serving as a cautionary tale about the grim political and economic fate awaiting other U.S. cities that put off or wish away their problems."

About Chicago's finances, Investors Business Daily recently reported: "(Chicago's) financial woes have mounted despite Emanuel's efforts to rein them in. Years, perhaps even decades, of past financial sins all seem to be coming home to roost now. ... Moody's Investors Service estimated in a 2013 report that fixed costs, like pension contributions and debt service, could soon eat up more than half the city's operating budget, up from about 15 percent of the 2015 budget."

With contributions to the city's pension plan for government workers funded at only 34 to 35 percent of their liability — and since unions resist any cuts or givebacks — taxes must be a raised to cover the shortfall. Raise taxes on job creators, and they leave. When they leave, they take their taxes with them, contributing to the city's further decline, the so-called "economic death spiral."

Nationwide, 10 percent of all parents have their kids in private schools. In Chicago, 39 percent of public school teachers with school-age children have their kids in private school.

So, what to do? Why, find people from whom more taxes can be extracted, of course. As former Rep. Barney Frank, D-Mass., once put it, "There are a lot of very rich people out there who we can tax."

Economist Stephen Moore writes: "Massachusetts Sen. Elizabeth Warren appeared on one of the late night talk shows last week, beating the class warfare drum and arguing for billions of dollars in new social programs paid for with higher taxes on millionaires and billionaires. In recent years, though, blue states such as California, Illinois, Delaware, Connecticut, Hawaii, Maryland and Minnesota adopted this very strategy, and they raised taxes on their wealthy residents. How did it work out? Almost all of these states lag behind the national average in growth of jobs and incomes. So, if income redistribution policies are the solution to shrinking the gap between rich and poor, why do they fail so miserably in the states?"

When French President Francois Hollande imposed a 75 percent tax on the rich, the rich said adieu. The revenue from his "rich person's tax" fell well short of projections. Turns out, rich people aren't stupid, French or otherwise. But the lessons of France are lost on Chicago. The lessons of Chicago are lost on the American left.

Hollywood Actors and Economics 101

April 23, 2015

Welcome to Hollywood, where dreams become real — and where logic, reason and economics 101 become dreams.

Take the current battle over the minimum wage. In Los Angeles County, the minimum wage is $9 per hour. Theater actors, however, can be paid as little as $7 a performance, and an actor can even work long rehearsal hours with no pay. Three decades ago, L.A. County actors sued their union for an exception to union wages for theaters with 99 seats or fewer seats.

Why do these stage actors work for so little? They want to work. By working they improve their skills, stay sharp and or perhaps have a chance to get spotted by an agent. Some say simply having something to do is better than just sitting around and waiting for a casting agent to call.

Actors Equity, the national union, wants to change this.

According to The New York Times: "The union, seizing a moment when organized labor is having some success pressuring low-wage employers to pay higher salaries, says many of this city's small theaters — which currently pay actors nothing for rehearsals, and stipends as low as $7 per (hour for) performances — should start paying California's minimum wage of $9 an hour." But then a very Republican thing happened — 66 percent of the union members voted against a higher minimum wage. Their rationale was simple. A higher minimum wage means fewer plays get performed. Fewer plays means fewer opportunities for actors and therefore fewer opportunities to gain experience, stay in practice or possibly get discovered. But the union's national council ignored this advisory vote and ordered, with some exceptions, a $9 per hour minimum wage.

When it comes to their own lives, these actors understand the law of economics: Artificially raise the cost of a good ?- in this case the price of an actor in a stage play ?- and you reduce the demand for actors.

Meanwhile, last year actor Kevin Spacey lobbied Maryland lawmakers to extend their tax credit program. He films his Netflix series, "House of Cards," in Maryland. That state offers generous tax credits and relaxed union rules, so that the Netflix series earned more money than would be the case if they filmed, for example, in Hollywood.

In Maryland, a production company can claim a credit on their income taxes equivalent to 25 to 27 percent of the costs of their film or TV production. If the credit is larger than a company's tax liability, the company can receive a refund from the state. "Maryland has capped the total value of credits it offers," writes the Washington Post, "with the amount varying by year but averaging about $12.5 million. Ten productions have been approved for credits since 2012. But the vast majority of the $62.5 million in funding has been allotted to 'House of Cards' ($37.6 million) and 'Veep' ($22.7 million)."

Hollywood studios aggressively seek tax credits and other benefits when determining where to shoot a television series or movie. When a shoot takes place other than Hollywood, studios call the out-of-state production a "runaway production." Brilliant marketing. Hollywood says, "We don't want to shoot outside of California, but, you see, our hands are tied. We have no choice. The production 'ran away' from us, lured by text credits and generous union rules." When a manufacturer, however, decides to move a facility to a different location ?- to take advantage of tax breaks — critics call this "outsourcing."

When it comes to politics, the Hollywood community votes for the party that seeks to raise both the minimum wage and taxes on the rich. The foundation of wealth redistribution is imposing higher and higher taxes on the so-called rich.

Yet after pulling the lever for the tax-hike party, the Hollywood community demands tax breaks for its own industry. A higher minimum wage is an article of faith for Democrats, whose party believes that society "exploits" poor workers. Democratic Party chair Debbie Wasserman Schultz says: "A raise of the federal minimum wage is one of those common-sense proposals that is both good for the economy and good for the country. ... This is a good first step to show we are committed to helping Americans who work hard and play by the rules. And as we tend to this core American value, we will expand the middle class, which will always be the backbone of this nation's economy. These principles are essential to Democrats like me, but they do not have to be exclusive to Democrats. We would welcome Republicans to join us in the achievement of improving wages and creating new momentum for the U.S. economy."

Another Hollywood denizen, Pat Sajak, the host of "Wheel of Fortune," recently offered a different perspective on the minimum wage. Sajak tweeted, "When I had minimum wage jobs, my goal was to better myself, not to better the minimum wage."

Tell People They're Victims — They'll Act Like Victims

April 30, 2015

In watching Baltimore burn, "progressives" run out of scapegoats. Over a week ago, a black man named Freddie Gray died after being arrested by police. Videotape shows Gray being dragged into a police van. Within a less than half an hour, his spine was somehow severed and he died seven days later.

Did an officer or the officers intentionally or inadvertently cause the injury? Did the vehicle suddenly stop, causing a possibly untethered or poorly tethered suspect/passenger to break his neck? Why was Gray stopped in the first place? Given that he ran from the police, did this provide a basis for pursuit, search and arrest? Does this not underscore the importance of police body cams and car-dash cams?

These are, of course, legitimate questions. And, in addition to the Baltimore police investigation, the Department of Justice announced that it, too, would examine the circumstances surrounding Gray's death.

So, why riot? Unlike Ferguson, where riots also took place, black Baltimore residents do not lack political power and representation. The mayor is black. The police commissioner and deputy commissioner are black. The police department is approximately 40 percent black, in a city with a black population of 63 percent. The new head of the Department of Justice, Loretta Lynch, is a black female, the second consecutive black person to run the Department of Justice. And, of course, the president of United States is black.

There's every reason, therefore, to believe that the investigations will be full, complete and thorough. This does not mean that the results will please everyone, but that the examination will be fair and open. After all, if a wildly popular mayor who received 84 percent of the vote cannot be trusted, who can?

This isn't Mississippi in 1955, where Emmett Till, a 14-year-old boy, was brutally murdered, only to have the obviously guilty killers acquitted by an all-white jury. This is not the 60s of white-run cities, with nearly all-white police departments policing all-black communities. In New York City, for example, most officers are people of color. Los Angeles had back-to-back black police chiefs, and as with New York City, the majority of L.A.'s street cops are people of color or women.

And it is not true, as some protestors claim, that "it doesn't happen the other way around." In Mobile, Alabama, in 2012, a black police officer shot and killed a white teenager. The white teen, high on drugs, was completely nude, and still the officer — fearing for his life — shot and killed the suspect. An investigation cleared the cop and — despite public pressure — a grand jury refused to indict him. No cameras. No CNN.

Just two days after Ferguson police officer Darren Wilson shot and killed Michael Brown in Ferguson, Missouri, a "not white" cop in Salt Lake City, Utah, shot and killed an unarmed 20-year-old man whose race has been described as Hispanic. The family of the dead man believes that the cop is a murderer. No cameras. No CNN.

So, why riot in Baltimore? The answer is that for some people facts and reason don't matter. It's about anger, excitement, disruption. Some call it a "subculture." Others say these are "at-risk youth." Still others call it the "underclass." But the 800-pound elephant in the room is the absence of fathers — responsible, involved fathers. Obama has said that a child growing up without a father is 20 times more likely to end up in jail. Today over 70 percent of black children are born to unwed mothers compared to 25 percent in the 1965.

To earn their near-monolithic 95-percent black vote, the Democratic Party repeatedly tells blacks of their continued oppression. During the 2012 election, Democratic National Committee chair, Debbie Wasserman Schultz, accused Republicans of seeking to "literally drag us all the way back to Jim Crow laws."

So, when a questionable white cop/black suspect takes place, some people, conditioned to react with anger and distrust, lash out. — it's "us against them" and "they are trying to oppress us."

Come election time, Democrats fan and exploit this anger. Rep. Charlie Rangel, D-N.Y., for example, made this accusation in his last race: "Everything we believe in, everything we believe in (Republicans) hate. They don't disagree — they hate. ... Some of them believe that slavery isn't over and that they won the Civil War." This is how Democrats get 95 percent of blacks to vote one way -? by telling them the other side is evil, that "the system" is corrupt and racist. So when a Freddy Gray, in police custody, turns up dead under suspicious circumstances, some will take to the streets to vent that "slavery isn't over."

Yes, Martin Luther King Jr. said, "A riot is the language of the unheard." When he said that, none of America's major cities had a black mayor. The country did not have back-to-back black attorneys general. The country did not have a black president elected — and reelected.? Baltimore's riot is the tragic language of modern welfare state.

Baltimore: The Intersection of the Grievance Culture and the Welfare State

May 7, 2015

After the mysterious death of suspect Freddie Gray, the Maryland state's attorney for Baltimore charged all six Baltimore police officers involved with his arrest and transport. The crimes ranging from "second-degree depraved-heart murder" to involuntary manslaughter, assault, misconduct in office and false imprisonment. Locals cheered her decision to charge all six. The charges followed three days of riots triggered by Gray's funeral and came almost immediately after the medical examiner filed his report calling Gray's death a "homicide."

Now for the hard part.

Not only will the charges be difficult to prove but three of those charged are black. The claim of illegal "racial profiling" argues that white racist officers possess an unwarranted fear of young black men. But what happens to that analysis when the accused officers are black? If black cops are just as likely to engage in race-based misconduct, why did Ferguson demonstrators demand a "diverse" police force?

If the Ferguson outrage and riots were about "lack of representation" or "lack of voice," this cannot be said about Baltimore. The city council is majority black, the police department is approximately 40 percent black, the top two officials running the department are black men, the city has a black mayor, the state's attorney for Baltimore City — who charged the six officers — is black, the new U.S. attorney general is a black female, and of course the President of the United States is black.

The left has created a culture of anger and entitlement based upon government dependency and the false assertion that racism remains a major problem. Rep. Hank Johnson, D-Ga., for example, said that the recent police killings mean "open season on black men in America." The Baltimore mayor's shameful embrace of the Rev. Al Sharpton, the race-hustling incendiary who demanded an arrest of Ferguson police officer Darren Wilson, did not help matters. Some actually believe this tripe about "institutional racism." Of those, how many rioted over Freddie Gray's "murder," no matter the race of the mayor?

Police shootings over the last several decades are *down*. Cop shootings of blacks are down more than 75 percent over the last 45 years, while the death-by-cop rate for whites has increased slightly. According to the CDC — which tracks all causes of death, including shootings by law enforcement — over twice as many whites are killed by police as are blacks.

Police "profile" because out of a relatively small percentage of the population come more than 50 percent of homicides and 40 percent of the people behind bars. Blacks are 13 percent of the population, but young blacks — the category that disproportionately commits crime — are 3 percent of the population.

Speaking of "root causes," Baltimore has not had a Republican mayor since 1967. So why haven't the Democrats addressed the "root causes"? In 1992, then-presidential candidate Bill Clinton blamed the "Rodney King riots" in Los Angeles on "12 years of denial and neglect" under the Reagan/Bush presidencies. Can we similarly attribute Baltimore's riots to six years of Obama's "progressive" policies?

Baltimore, Democrats say, needs a "new Marshall plan." But, according to the Heritage Foundation, we have spent over $22 trillion on anti-poverty programs. On education in Baltimore, in 2012 (the latest year available), they spent $15,287 per student. Yet almost half of urban Baltimoreans fail to graduate high school, and of those who do, many cannot read write and compute at grade level. Spend more?

In 1965, 25 percent of black kids were born out of wedlock. Today that number is up to 72 percent. Obama said that a kid without a father is 20 times more likely to go to jail. Blame the welfare state that incentivizes women into marrying the government.

Last year 189 blacks were killed in Baltimore. Where were CNN and President Barack Obama and then-Attorney General Eric Holder and Sharpton? Chicago averages 35 to 40 murders per month, the majority by and against blacks — and most remain unsolved. Where are CNN/Obama/Holder/Sharpton?

Obama has now misfired in at least four "racial" matters: the Cambridge police/Harvard professor incident; Trayvon Martin/George Zimmerman; Michael Brown/Darren Wilson; and now Baltimore.

Obama's claimed the "Cambridge police acted stupidly" in arresting black Harvard professor Henry Louis Gates Jr., who falsely and belligerently accused a white officer of racial profiling.

In the case of Trayvon Martin, Obama said, "If I had a son, he'd look like Trayvon." But the jury found Zimmerman not only not guilty, but jurors later said that during their deliberations race never came up.

In the case of Ferguson, the Department of Justice found that Michael Brown very likely did not have his hands up and that the cop acted appropriately when he killed Brown, a charging suspect who posed a risk of death or serious injury.

Who would've thought that after the election and reelection of the nation's first black president, we'd see race riots in our nation's cities? Baltimore is what happens at the intersection of the grievance culture and the welfare state.

Illinois State Sen. Barack Obama's 'Urban Agenda'

May 14, 2015

After the recent Baltimore riots, left-wing critics accused President Barack Obama of lacking an "urban agenda." Critics like PBS's hard lefty Tavis Smiley said: "What do we see in Baltimore and Ferguson and beyond? Racism, poverty and militarism. And so poverty is clearly connected to this. My sense is that this is going to become the new normal. These kinds of uprisings and riots are going to happen a lot more if we can't get serious about jobs, jobs, jobs with a living wage for all fellow citizens. ...

"My problem with the President so far, respectfully, is that he has had a sort of 'hands off' approach to a 'hands up' crisis, and I don't think that's the answer to the prayer, either. ... When you have police killings that are on the rise ... for me, that's a problem; that's a pandemic. I think that our leaders ought to call a state of emergency ... from the President on down. We can then, I think, get a real conversation about police accountability, about civilian oversight and, again, about jobs for fellow citizens."

Black Princeton professor Dr. Cornel West said of Obama: "Maybe he couldn't do that much. But at least tell the truth. I would rather have a white president fundamentally dedicated to eradicating poverty and enhancing the plight of working people than a black president tied to Wall Street and drones."

But as a local Illinois lawmaker, then-state Sen. Barack Obama did, in fact, enact an "urban" agenda on education and housing.

Bill Ayers, the former fugitive and still unrepentant domestic terrorist/member of the Weather Underground turned educator, founded the Chicago Annenberg Challenge with a $50 million grant from the Annenberg Foundation. Just three years out of law school, Obama chaired the newly formed CAC board from 1995 to 1999, spending millions to "improve" Chicago public schools. In all, CAC distributed more than $100 million from 1995 to 2001 to improve Chicago schools.

Rather than fund the schools directly, Ayers required schools to work with "external partners," who focused on political radicalism. "External partners" that focused on math or science were turned down. The CAC instead funded groups like the far-left Association of Community Organizations for Reform Now or the South Shore African Village Collaborative and the Dual Language Exchange, which focused on Afrocentricity, anti-capitalism, political consciousness and bilingualism.

After six years, what did the CAC achieve? By its own assessment, the money was wasted. Their report said: "There were no statistically significant differences in student achievement between Annenberg schools and demographically similar non-Annenberg schools. This indicates that there was no Annenberg effect on achievement."

What about housing? Surely Illinois state Sen. Obama has something to show for his public-private partnership agenda to improve public housing? During his eight-year service in the state house, from 1997 through 2004, Obama co-wrote a state law pooling tax credits for development projects. Then and current adviser Valerie Jarrett served as the chief executive of Habitat Company, which managed a project called Grove Parc Plaza from 2001 to 2008.

Grove Parc Plaza, a renamed redevelopment of an older housing project, was opened in 1990 with a new owner, with funding from the federal government. A private management firm was hired to oversee the property, which lay in state Sen. Obama's district. After losing the contract in 2001 to Habitat, the head of the original management company was convicted of embezzling $1 million in management fees.

Residents complained about deteriorating conditions. By 2006, after repeated warnings, federal inspectors found conditions so bad and repairs so minimal they moved to seize Grove Parc, later demolishing it.

Similarly, Rezmar Corp., cofounded in 1989 by Tony Rezko, used more than $87 million in government grants, loan and credits over the next nine years to renovate and manage 1,000 apartments in 30 Chicago buildings — 11 of them in Obama's district. Residents complained of rats, insect infestations, no heat, leaking windows and piles of trash. By the time Obama entered the state Senate, buildings were deteriorating and Chicago was suing Rezmar for various violations.

Rezmar got out of the subsidized housing game and — apparently with plenty still left in their bank account — got into high-end developments. Rezko, the Obama friend and political supporter who helped the Obamas purchase their Chicago home in 2005, was indicted in 2006 on federal charges of wire fraud, bribery, money laundering and attempted extortion. He was ultimately convicted on 16 charges and received a 10 1/2-year sentence.

So to his left-wing critics, Obama could legitimately say that as a local lawmaker, he did implement his urban agenda on housing and education. That agenda was simple: spend more taxpayer money. Never mind that America already spends more money, K-12, than all but Switzerland, Norway and Luxembourg. Unless families embrace and emphasize education, spending more just wastes taxpayer money. As to housing, that's the private sector's job. The real lesson of the Wall Street-housing meltdown is that government never should have been in the housing business.

But, no, let's spend more, no matter the outcome.

George Clintonopoulos!

May 21, 2015

What took so long?

The question isn't whether George Stephanopoulos compromised his credentials as a "journalist" by failing to reveal his donations to the Clinton Foundation. The question is why, immediately after Stephanopoulos left the Clinton administration, ABC hired this partisan in the first place.

In 1996, when ABC hired him, the initial press release said he would "serve both as a political analyst and as a correspondent." The "correspondent" role caused such an uproar — even in liberal mainstream media — that a few days later ABC quickly retreated: "I don't know how that got into the press release," said a spokeswoman. "He will not report the news."

Then-ABC News Vice President Joanna Bistany said Stephanopoulos would be a commentator like ABC contributor William Kristol, Republican Dan Quayle's former chief of staff. "I view it the same way as Kristol," she said. "He has a point of view, a political persuasion." Bistany also said, "We want a mix of voices," assuring that Stephanopoulos wouldn't "do anything that has any appearance of conflict."

Then came the double cross.

By 1999, Stephanopoulos was a regular contributor on "World News Tonight" and "Good Morning America" and had co-anchored ABC's overnight news program. Still, ABC assured viewers that he'd stay away from partisan political stories. "We're all conscious of the sensitivity with him having been part of the news in Washington," said then-ABC News President David Westin. "We wouldn't have him be the beat reporter on the (Al) Gore campaign."

An ABC spokeswoman added, "He will not be the beat reporter assigned to a campaign," although that "does not mean that we won't have him doing more general political stories."

In 2002, Stephanopoulos became host of "This Week," and two years later ABC named him "chief Washington correspondent."

Now comes the news that Stephanopoulos gave $75,000 to the Clinton Foundation but failed to disclose the contribution to his employer and to his viewers. He offered this apology: "Those donations were a matter of public record, but I should have made additional disclosures on-air when we covered the foundation, and I now believe that directing personal donations to that foundation was a mistake. ... I should have gone the extra mile to avoid even the appearance of a conflict. I apologize to all of you for failing to do that."

Stephanopoulos, however, has yet to publicly disclose further ties to the Clinton Foundation. He served several times as a panelist, moderator or "featured attendee" for the foundation. Also, the Washington Free Beacon reports that Hillary Clinton's campaign manager, Robby Mook, once worked as an intern for Stephanopoulos when he briefly taught at Columbia.

Did ABC not see the political documentary "The War Room"? Filmmakers, during the 1992 presidential campaign, followed Bill Clinton's top campaign advisers, James Carville and Stephanopoulos. Both were passionate political operatives. Stephanopoulos, for example, aggressively defended Clinton against charges of infidelity and of lacking "character." Consider this exchange with ABC's Sam Donaldson:

Donaldson: "Now, Gov. Clinton has a character problem, but I take it that your line of counterattack is that it's—"

Stephanopoulos: "Gov. Clinton has no character problem. He's passed his character tests."

Donaldson: "Well, I mean, he has not denied that he has engaged in marital infidelity. He denied a specific one—"

Stephanopoulos: "He has said that he had problems in his marriage."

Donaldson: "That's right. And he has talked about the draft, and to some people it's a character problem."

Stephanopoulos: "Bill Clinton's passed his character test throughout his life and throughout this campaign. ... (The American people) don't want to be diverted by side issues, and they're not going to let the Republican attack machine divert them."

After the '92 election, Stephanopoulos served as White House communications director and senior adviser on policy and strategy. During Clinton's Monica Lewinsky/perjury scandal, a Time magazine cover showed a grim president with his equally grim domestic policy adviser Stephanopoulos. The headline read: "Deep Water: How the President's men tried to hinder the Whitewater investigation."

Stephanopoulos' recent grilling of "Clinton Cash" author Peter Schweizer becomes all the more brazen given Stephanopoulos' own then-undisclosed 75K contribution to the Clinton Foundation. Schweizer's book questions whether donors received favors from then-Secretary of State Hillary Clinton. Stephanopoulos repeatedly asked whether he had "evidence" or any kind of "smoking gun."

Carole Simpson, a former colleague at ABC, was blunt: "There's a coziness that George cannot escape. ... While he did try to separate himself from his political background to become a journalist, he really is not a journalist."

When Stephanopoulos apologized for failing to disclose his contributions, he said he should have avoided "even the appearance of a conflict." Doesn't this standard apply to Clinton Foundation donors and Hillary Clinton's job as secretary of state? Doesn't this standard also apply to ABC and Stephanopoulos' job as news "correspondent" or "anchor"?

Finally, why, during all these years that ABC fraudulently passed off Stephanopoulos as a journalist, did real journalists say nothing?

All Gave Some, Some Gave All —
Memorial Day Salute

May 28, 2015

On November 11, 2011, Congress voted to award a Congressional Gold Medal for the 20,000 black Marines of Montford Point, the first blacks to serve as Marines. I write about Staff Sgt. Elder — and my struggle to understand him — in my latest book, "Dear Father, Dear Son."

On August 13, 2013, Col. Jason Bohm, commander, "Fighting 5th," United States Marine Corps, Camp Pendleton, made the following remarks:

"We are honored that you joined us today to recognize the service of one of our own, Staff Sgt. Randolph Elder. ...

"In the days leading up to World War II, the United States was a segregated society, in which the African-American Community faced bigotry, racial prejudice and discrimination. It was not until June 25, 1941, just five months before the bombing of Pearl Harbor thrust us into the Second World War, that President Franklin D. Roosevelt issued an executive order, No. 8802, that first opened the door for African-Americans to serve in all branches of the armed services. ...

"But even with this direction, the Marine Corps was slow to embrace bringing African-Americans into its ranks. In fact, many doubted whether African-Americans would meet the high standards the Marine Corps was known for. There was little doubt how some in the Marine Corps felt about accepting these men into the corps when the commandant at the time stated, 'The Negro race has every opportunity now to satisfy its aspirations for combat in the army, a very much larger organization than the Navy or Marine Corps. And their desire to enter the naval service is largely, I think, to break into a club that doesn't want them.'

"Regardless of the commandant's protest, our nation's civilian leadership saw the need for equity in allowing African-Americans to serve proudly in the nation's naval service, and announced in April, 1942, that a battalion of 900 African-Americans would be formed in the Marine Corps once suitable training sites were established. The battalion would be organized into a composite defense battalion, consisting of coastal defense artillery, antiaircraft artillery, tanks and infantry, to defend overseas bases like those of Wake, Johnston and Midway Islands they had already seen action against Japanese forces in the opening salvos of World War II. ...

"The first recruits were used to build the now-famous camp of wooden huts (at Montford Point, near what soon became known as Camp Lejeune), so others could follow and begin their training. Soon they will all be braving a variety of threats — ranging from the swagger sticks of tough drill instructors to the snakes, mosquitoes and bears that inhabited the area. As the camp was built, the call went out and the country's African-American communities responded.

"Recruits start to pile in, from the North and from the South, from all walks of life. They came for different reasons. Some wanted the challenge of being a Marine. Some wanted to earn a living. But they all came to serve their country honorably, regardless of still being treated like second-class citizens. Randolph Elder was one of these men. ...

"(He) was born in Athens, Georgia, in 1915. And he grew up during the Great Depression. He would work a number of odd jobs, such as being a bellboy, a shoe-shiner, a valet and a cook before becoming a porter on the railroad and getting his first taste of California. Like many Americans at the outbreak of World War II, Randolph Elder chose to serve his country. But he wouldn't settle for any service. He wanted to be one of the best. Although he knew it would be challenging, Randolph enlisted in the Marine Corps and would be sent to Montford Point, where he would earn the title of Marine.

"Based on past job experience, Pvt. Elder, at the time, was made a cook, a job critically important to the Marine Corps — because any

Marine will tell you that there are two things you don't mess with: a Marine's pay and his chow. Living up to the ethos of the corps, of every Marine's a rifleman and a fighter — regardless of what their primary job is — Pvt. Elder was trained for combat and sent overseas to the Pacific theater to prepare for the expected invasion of Japan. He would spend his time in the Pacific on the island of Guam, and performed so well he was promoted four times, attaining the rank of staff sergeant.

"Having gone through a time of racism and bigotry, Randolph Elder overcame. He would raise his sons to understand that the sky's the limit, and they should follow their dreams. But his legacy goes beyond that of his immediate family. The hard work, superior performance and professionalism of Staff Sgt. Elder and his fellow Montford Point Marines broke down the barriers and opened the doors to future generations of African-Americans, resulting in a Marine Corps today in which one is judged on the value they bring to the table, not by their race, color or gender."

Semper fi.

$15 Minimum Wage: Women, Blacks Hurt Most

June 4, 2015

Fourteen to one, in favor.

That was the Los Angeles City Council vote to raise, over the next five years, the city's minimum wage from $9 an hour to $15. Of course, as Investor's Business Daily tells us, the $15 per hour really is closer to $20.

How does it get to $20?

Investor's Business Daily says: "Once all the nonwage costs are added, including payroll taxes, paid sick leave and the big one — ObamaCare's employer mandate — minimum compensation for a full-time worker could rise as high as $19.28 an hour by 2020, an IBD analysis finds. That would amount to a jump of $10.67, or 124 percent, since June 2014."

How cynical is the push for higher minimum wage?

The Association of Community Organizations for Reform Now, traveled from state to state, collecting signatures to place minimum wage increase initiatives on ballots. To pull this off, the organization needed to hire lots of workers. In 1995, ACORN came to California to gather signatures for a higher minimum wage. But ACORN sued the state, seeking to exempt itself from California's minimum wage and overtime laws. Its brief read, "The more ACORN must pay each individual outreach worker — either because of minimum wage or overtime requirements — the fewer outreach workers it will be able to hire."

Not cynical enough?

Union leaders, who successfully lobbied for LA's $15-an-hour minimum wage, then asked for an exemption for any firms using union labor! Repeat, the very same union leaders who successfully lobbied for a $15-an-hour minimum wage, then wanted an exemption for businesses that employ union labor and negotiate their wages under collective bargaining. Union bosses want the fear of a $15 minimum wage hike to push companies into unionizing their labor forces.

This push for higher minimum wage will mostly hurt women — a constituency that the left claims to care so much about. According to the National Women's Law Center, women are at least half of the minimum-wage workers in all 50 states. In New Hampshire, Arkansas, Maine and Pennsylvania, 70 percent of the minimum wage workers are female.

Before the ever-increasing minimum wage laws took effect, a black teenager was slightly more likely to be employed than a white teenager. Economist Walter Williams writes: "In the 1940s and 1950s ... teenage unemployment among blacks was slightly lower than among whites, and black teens were more active in the labor force as well. All of my classmates, friends, and acquaintances who wanted to work found jobs of one sort or another."

Minimum wage and other New Deal policies, according to CATO's Jim Powell, cost jobs: "The flagship of the New Deal was the National Industrial Recovery Act, passed in June 1933. It authorized the president to issue executive orders establishing some 700 industrial cartels, which restricted output and forced wages and prices above market levels. The minimum wage regulations made it illegal for employers to hire people who weren't worth the minimum because they lacked skills. As a result, some 500,000 blacks, particularly in the South, were estimated to have lost their jobs."

Today's push for a higher minimum wage occurs as the supposed "pay gap" between male and female millennials now approaches extinction. Pew Research Center says: "(T)oday's young women are the first in modern history to start their work lives at near parity with men. In 2012, among workers ages 25 to 34, women's hourly earnings were 93 percent those of men. ... And women in the younger age cohort were significantly more likely than their male counterparts to have completed a bachelor's degree ?- 38 percent versus 31 percent in 2013."

Two years ago, Elissa Shevinsky, described as a "social justice warrior," complained about "sexism" in high-tech industries. She argued for policies to encourage more women in tech. But Shevinsky later had an epiphany: "I think the more important meaning is to actively choose a path that's yours — for women to create their own companies and their own infrastructures, to actively seek out people and create places that are a fit for them. Women are martyring themselves trying to change the existing culture, and it's miserable for everyone."

In other words, stop acting like victicrats — and take control. Shevinsky now says, "Complaining can be effective but also authoritarian, and often unpleasant for everyone involved. Building something new can be even more impactful, and I believe it's a healthier approach."

Former Sony Pictures co-chief Amy Pascal gives equally blunt advice about knowing and getting what you're worth. After the Sony cyberattack revealed that the studio head paid star Jennifer Lawrence less money than her less-popular male costars, Pascal offered this defense: "Here's the problem. I run a business. People want to work for less money; I'll pay them less money. I don't call them up and say, 'Can I give you some more?' Because that's not what you do when you run a business. The truth is, what women have to do is not work for less money. They have to walk away. People shouldn't be so grateful for jobs. ... People should know what they're worth."

Any questions?

Obama Hearts Private School — For Himself and Family

June 11, 2015

Barack Obama, for his own education, never set foot in a public school.

When he was 10 years of age, his mother shipped him back from Indonesia to his grandparents in Hawaii so that young Barack could get a first-class American education. He entered Punahou, the expensive and most prestigious prep school in the islands. From there, despite his admittedly indifferent grades, Obama was admitted to Occidental, an elite private college in Los Angeles. He spent two years there, after which he transferred to Columbia University, one of the private Ivy League schools. After Columbia, Obama attended Harvard Law, another private Ivy League school.

What about Michelle, then Michelle Robinson? Doesn't she often brag that she attended public schools? But her public school cheerleading requires an asterisk. True, Michelle attended a public high school. But it was Chicago's first magnet school, and admission was a selective and highly competitive process. Michelle spent close to three hours each day on a bus to escape her subpar local public school. So Michelle, in essence, attended an exclusive high school, an option available to her because of her proactive, pro-education parents and her willingness to sacrifice the time to go to and from this superior school.

What about the Obama's own children? Surely the children of a pro-public school politician would attend public schools as a seal of approval. On the contrary, the children of then-Sen. Obama attended a private school operated by the University of Chicago, where

Obama had taught as an instructor in the law school. This job enabled the Obama girls to go at little or no cost to Obama.

After Obama was elected president and preparing to move to Washington, D.C., Michelle Obama engaged in a public search for an appropriate school for their children. Michelle considered public schools in D.C. "There are some terrific individual schools in the D.C. system," her husband said later.

But, come time for enrollment, the Obamas chose Sidwell Friends, a private Quaker school whose most famous recent grad is Chelsea Clinton. Annual tuition? Almost $40,000 a year, and this excludes books and other material.

Democrats, of course, argue that we need to "invest" more in education. We already spend more on education, K-12, than any other country with the exception of Switzerland, Norway and Luxembourg.

Back in 1985, a federal judge decided to take a different approach, instead of mandating cross-town busing in Kansas City. Why not make urban schools so attractive that all students, no matter their race, would want to go there? He ordered the school district to build what many called "world-class public schools."

And spend they did.

The district built 15 new schools. Then it equipped dozens of magnet schools with equipment and personnel for state-of-the-art academic, athletic and arts programs. One elementary school offered private Suzuki violin lessons for every student. A middle school hired 10 "resource teachers" to develop projects in specialty subjects. Kansas City added a Montessori kindergarten and a first-grade Spanish immersion program. Some teachers got raises, while others received reduced workloads.

At a time when most Americans didn't have a PC or an Apple Macintosh, one Kansas City high school boasted 900 top-of-the-line computers. Others had an Olympic-sized swimming pool complete with six diving boards, a padded wrestling room, a classical Greek theater, an eight-lane indoor track and a professionally equipped gymnastics center. Some of the renovations included a robotics lab, TV studios, a zoo, a planetarium and a wildlife sanctuary. Instead of using buses to bring white kids to the inner-city schools, the district hired 120 taxis.

After 15 years and $2 billion dollars, the Kansas City school district failed all of Missouri's 11 academic performance standards and became the first big-city school district to lose its academic accreditation. All that spending managed to attract several hundred white suburban students in the early 1990s, but many later left.

This brings us to vouchers, where the money follows the student — rather than the other way around.

Urban parents want the option to remove their kid from an underperforming local government school to a better school. Polls show 80 percent of inner-city parents want vouchers. In Philadelphia, 44 percent of public-school teachers with school-age children send their kids to a private school. In Chicago, it's 39 percent. Nationwide, about 11 percent of all parents enroll their children in private schools; only 6 percent of black parents do so.

A year and a half after the Obama girls had settled into their new school, Obama was asked whether any D.C. public schools offered his daughters the same quality of education as a private school. "I'll be blunt with you," said Obama. "The answer is 'no' right now." But then he added, "Given my position, if I wanted to find a great public school for Malia and Sasha to be in, we could probably maneuver to do it. But the broader problem is for a mom or a dad who are working hard but don't have a bunch of connections." So it's who you know, how much clout you have.

Obama does not realize it, but he made an open-and-shut case for vouchers.

Father's Day: Being Raised Without a Father Is Not a Death Sentence

June 18, 2015

I wrote my latest book, "Dear Father, Dear Son: Two Lives, Eight Hours," to personalize the biggest issue facing the country — the growing number of fatherless homes, particularly in the black community, where over 70 percent of children are born to unwed mothers.

Being raised without a father is hard. One is more likely to drop out, be unemployed or end up in jail. But it's not a death sentence. The book is about what my father faced and overcame: Only child; irresponsible, illiterate mother; never met his biological father; born in Jim Crow South; kicked out of his house at age 13 — never to return — all as the Great Depression began.

It doesn't get much worse than that.

He joined the Marines and became a Montford Point Marine — the first black Marines. A few years ago, Congress awarded the 20,000 Montford Point Marines a Congressional Medal. My dad had a private, posthumous ceremony at Camp Pendleton, California.

In the Marines, my dad was promoted four times, becoming a staff sergeant. He was in charge of the kitchen, but when he returned to the South after the war, he could not get a job as a cook. "We don't hire n—gers," he was told. "You have no references," some told him — which was just a more polite way of saying the same thing.

So he relocated to Los Angeles, a city he once visited when, before the war, he worked on the trains as a Pullman porter. But again, no one would hire him because he lacked "references." So Dad took two jobs as a janitor and cooked for a family on the weekends — while going to night school to get a GED.

But my dad was not bitter, never whined about what "the white man" did to him. He said the best weapon against racism was getting really good at what you do. He worked his butt off, and scraped up enough nickels and dimes to start a small restaurant in his late 40s, which he ran until his mid-80s.

He was a lifelong Republican. "Welfare was the worst thing that ever came down the pike," he said. He hated the way Democrats "played the race card" and offered "free stuff." Dad would say, "When you try to get something for nothing, you'll end up getting nothing for something."

As I wrote "Dear Father," I constantly asked him why he never became bitter, became a criminal or just simply dropped out of life. He looked at me as if I were insane. "What choice did I have?" he said. Becoming a criminal was "not an option."

He said when his mom kicked him out of the house, she stood on the porch and, as he walked down the road, yelled, "You'll be back — or end up in the penitentiary!"

He turned to me, held up his hand and proudly said, "I've never spent one minute in jail."

He repeatedly offered my two brothers and me his lessons-learned mantras: "Hard work wins." "You get out of life want you put into it." "You cannot control the outcome, but you 100 percent control the effort." "When things go wrong — as they will — before blaming others go to the nearest mirror and ask yourself, 'Did I do everything possible to change the outcome?'" And finally: "No matter how hard you work or how good you are, bad things will happen. How you respond to those bad things will tell your mother and me whether we raised a man."

A few years before Dad died, he and I were in his garage getting rid of things he no longer wanted. I came across an envelope with a note in it. "What's this?" I asked him. Turns out it was a letter he'd written to my then two-year-old older brother, Kirk. Dad, fearing if something happened to him, wanted to leave him a roadmap for life. Dad had forgotten about the letter:

"May 4, 1951

"Kirk, my Son, you are now starting out in life — a life that Mother and I cannot live for you.

"So as you journey through life, remember it's yours, so make it a good one. Always try to cheer up the other fellow.

"Learn to think straight, analyze things, be sure you have all the facts before concluding and always spend less than you earn.

"Make friends, work hard and play hard. Most important of all remember this — the best of friends wear out if you use them.

"This may sound silly, Son, but no matter where you are on the 29th of September (Kirk's birthday), see that Mother gets a little gift, if possible, along with a big kiss and a broad smile.

"When you are out on your own, listen and take advice but do your own thinking, and concluding, set up a reasonable goal, then be determined to reach it. You can and will, it's up to you, Son.

"Your Father,
"Randolph Elder"

The Meaning of Charleston

June 25, 2015

Almost immediately after a white killer gunned down nine black worshippers at a historic church in Charleston, South Carolina, out came the politics.

On the Capitol grounds in Columbia flies the battlefield flag of Gen. Robert E. Lee's Army of Northern Virginia, often erroneously called the "Confederate flag." Right after the shooting, calls came for the flag's removal. South Carolina Gov. Nikki Haley, until now, had defended the compromise that moved the flag in 2000 from the Capitol dome, where it had flown since 1962, to a nearby Confederate soldier memorial on the statehouse grounds.

The killer did not pull out a Confederate flag and use it to kill people. He used a .45. Also, he had flags of apartheid South Africa and separatist Rhodesia. Ban them, too?

President Barack Obama took the opportunity to make the case for additional gun control legislation. "We don't have all the facts," he said, "but we do know that once again, innocent people were killed in part because someone who wanted to inflict harm had no trouble getting their hands on a gun."

OK, now that Obama mentions it, suppose one or more of the churchgoers had been armed? South Carolina is one of 40 states that allow citizens to carry a concealed weapon on a "shall issue" basis, meaning that as long as you pass that state's basic qualification requirements — things like age, training, no criminal history, etc. — the state will not deny you a permit to carry a concealed weapon.

Permit holders, however, cannot bring a firearm to a "house of worship." Whether the confessed Charleston killer, Dylann Roof, knew this, we don't know. We do know that one of Roof's friends said Roof wanted to attack a local college. But, according to the friend, Roof switched targets because of the security around the school. If the school security deterred the killer, might allowing concealed carry in a "house of worship" have a similar effect?

How about we spend a little time on whether someone could have and should have said something to someone? Roof apparently told people of his intentions to start a "race war" — and at least some friends knew he possessed a .45.

Obama said the tragedy reminds us "we've got a lot of work to do." He spoke of the 1963 church bombing in Birmingham, Alabama, where four black girls were killed and nearly two dozen people wounded.

But the differences between Birmingham in 1963 and Charleston in 2015 are staggering.

In 1963, Birmingham was home to one of the most virulent chapters of the KKK. Bombings of black properties were so frequent people referred to the city as "Bombingham." In fact, this church bombing was the third bombing to take place in that city since its public schools were forcibly desegregated just 11 days earlier.

Bull Connor, the commissioner of public safety, infamously sicced dogs and turned water hoses on civil rights workers. The governor, George Wallace, once stood in front of the state Capitol and shouted, "Segregation now, segregation tomorrow and segregation forever." The FBI was led by J. Edgar Hoover, who believed the civil rights movement was communist-inspired. Reportedly, the FBI knew fairly soon who had committed the bombing but sat on the information. It took decades before all of those involved were brought to justice. That was 1963.

Today the U.S. attorney general is a black woman, the second consecutive black person to hold the position. She called for a federal investigation of the Charleston shooting. South Carolina's governor is Nikki Haley, a woman of Indian descent. One of the state's U.S. senators is a black man, Tim Scott, the first black person from the South to serve in the Senate since four years after Reconstruction. Charleston's popular mayor has held the job for four decades and is respected by both black and white communities.

Does the racist Charleston killer represent a growing, threatening underbelly of American racism?

In 1969, Charles Manson, like the Charleston killer, wanted to start a "race war." Over the course of two nights, he ordered the murder of seven people. And Manson had a "family" of followers. The Charleston killer complained that he could recruit no help. Did we launch into a national soul search over whether Manson represented white racism? No, we placed him in the category of murderous, evil deviant — the same place to put the Charleston killer.

In 1960, 60 percent of Americans said they would "never" vote for a black president. In 2008, America elected a black man as president of the United States. A 2006 Los Angeles Times/Bloomberg poll found that only 4 percent of Democratic voters and 3 percent of Republican voters would not vote for a black president. Obama got a greater share of the "white vote" than even John Kerry did in 2004. Was Kerry a victim of racial discrimination?

This is not your grandfather's America.

SCOTUS: Congress Doesn't Want to 'Destroy' Our Health-Care System? Oh, Yes, It Does!

July 2, 2015

For the second time, Chief Justice John Roberts breathed life into Obamacare and rescued it from the Constitution.

In the first big Obamacare ruling, Roberts called Obamacare a "tax," and therefore lawfully enacted as consistent with the powers of Congress — and not a violation of the Commerce Clause. Never mind the Obama administration sold Obamacare with the assurance that individuals who failed to purchase health insurance would incur a penalty — not a tax.

On this latest ruling, Roberts takes the words "established by the State" to mean "established by the states or by the federal government" — even though the last five words appear nowhere in the law passed by Congress and signed by President Obama.

Obamacare's architect, Jonathan Gruber, admits on videotape the law was written this way by the feds to "squeeze" the states into setting up state-run health care exchanges — by offering tax credits to the citizens of those states *only* if their state set up an exchange. No state exchanges — meaning that state's citizens have to use the federal exchange — and no tax credits for you. That simple, that clear.

But Roberts argued, "Congress passed the Affordable Care Act to improve health insurance markets, not to destroy them." Thus, Roberts reasoned, the interpretation by the plaintiffs would erode, not preserve and expand, our health-care system.

On the contrary, Mr. Chief Justice — Obama and the Democrats have every intention of "destroying" our insurance-based health care system in favor of single payer or, as Rep. John Conyers, D-Mich., puts it, "Medicare for all."

In 2003, Obama, then an Illinois state senator, addressed an audience at a AFL-CIO conference on civil, human and women's rights: "I happen to be a proponent of a single-payer, universal health-care program. I see no reason why the United States of America, the wealthiest country in the history of the world, spending 14 percent of its gross national product on health care, cannot provide basic health insurance to everybody. ... A single-payer health care plan, a universal health-care plan. That's what I'd like to see. But as all of you know, we may not get there immediately. Because first we've got to take back the White House, we've got to take back the Senate, and we've got to take back the House."

The Las Vegas Sun headline was blunt: "(Sen. Harry) Reid (D-Nev.) Says Obamacare Just a Step Toward Eventual Single-Payer System." In an August, 2013, Las Vegas PBS-TV appearance, the then-Senate majority leader said we need to "work our way past" our insurance-based system: "What we've done with Obamacare is have a step in the right direction, but we're far from having something that's going to work forever." Asked whether Obamacare is just a stopgap on our way to that type of system, Reid said, "Yes, yes. Absolutely, yes." He added that he pushed for it in 2009: "We had a real good run at the public option. ...Don't think we didn't have a tremendous number of people who wanted a single-payer system."

Howard Dean, the former Democratic National Committee chair, also describes Obamacare as just a step toward the elimination of our insurance-based system in favor of single-payer. During the 2008 presidential campaign, Dean talked about the health-care proposals of Democratic candidates Barack Obama and Sen. Hillary Clinton, D-N.Y., and compared their proposals to that of Republican Sen. John McCain: "I think while someday we may end up with a single-payer system, it's clear that we're not going to do it all at once, so I think both candidates' health-care plans are a big step forward. Certainly compared to Sen. McCain, who represents a big step backward."

Does anyone *really* believe the Obamacare promises of quality, accessibility *and* low costs can be achieved while retaining our insurance-based system? Obamacare promised to add 30 million newly insured to Medicaid; force insurers to accept those with pre-existing illnesses; raise no taxes on the middle class to pay for it; force insurance carriers to allow "children" under the age of 26 to remain on their parents' policy; allow you to keep your doctor and your plan — if you chose to; disallow carriers from "discriminating" against men and women in setting prices; save the "typical family" $2,500 in premiums; and not "raise the deficit by one dime."

Even under Obama, there is no such thing as a free lunch. To pay for these government-imposed expenses, insurance carriers are seeking higher premiums while imposing higher deductibles and co-pays. Since health care is a "right," since Obamacare was to be "affordable" and since the greedy, nasty insurance companies seek profits, the left will then say, "We have no alternative. Medicare for all!"

So, yes, Mr. Justice Roberts, Democrats who passed Obamacare without a single Republican vote absolutely seek "to destroy" and "not improve health insurance markets." This is all according to plan.

Donald Trump Strikes a Nerve

July 9, 2015

Businessman and celebrity Donald Trump, in his nearly hour-long, teleprompter-less announcement of his GOP presidential candidacy, said: "The U.S. has become a dumping ground for everybody else's problems. ... When Mexico sends its people, they're not sending their best. They're not sending you. They're not sending you. They're sending people that have lots of problems, and they're bringing those problems with us. They're bringing drugs. They're bringing crime. They're rapists. And some, I assume, are good people."

His crude and over-the-top comment instantly made him the most hated white man since Donald Sterling. Never mind that Trump hit on a topic the media are loath to admit: our borders remain porous.

The backlash against Trump was fierce. NBC, which carried Trump's show, "The Apprentice," ended their relationship with him. Univision dropped Trump's Miss USA pageant. ESPN moved a golf tournament from a Trump-owned resort to another site. Macy's dropped Trump's menswear line. And New York's Mayor Bill de Blasio said, "We are reviewing Trump contracts with the city." For New York City, the Trump organization runs a carousel, an ice-skating rink and a golf course.

Former New York governor and Republican presidential candidate George Pataki also attacked Trump. Pataki sent a letter to about a dozen rivals for the GOP nomination urging them to denounce Trump.

Actress America "Ugly Betty" Ferrera said: "I heard what you said about the kind of people you think Latino immigrants are —

people with problems, who bring drugs, crime and rape to America. While your comments are incredibly ignorant and racist, I don't want to spend my time chastising you. I'll leave that to your business partners like Univision and NBC, who have the power to scold you where it hurts. Instead, I'm writing to say thank you! You see, what you just did with your straight talk was send more Latino voters to the polls than several registration rallies combined!"

But polls show most Americans believe that our borders are not only porous — but are porous *by design*. According to a January Rasmussen poll: "Most U.S. voters think the Mexican government doesn't do enough to stop illegal immigration and drug trafficking and favor stopping foreign aid to our southern neighbor. ... Just 14 percent of likely U.S. voters think the Mexican government wants to stop its citizens from illegally entering the United States. ... Fifty-five percent say Mexico is not interested in stopping illegal immigration."

Within days of Trump's comments, two women, one in Texas and one in California, were murdered by illegal aliens. In the case of the California woman, she was out on a walk with her father in a popular tourist area of San Francisco. She was shot and killed by an illegal alien who had been previously deported five times and convicted of felonies seven times, but was nevertheless out, free and on the streets. Immigration and Customs Enforcement claims they placed a detainer order on the illegal alien.

But San Francisco is a so-called "sanctuary city," meaning that unless the feds have a court order or warrant demanding that the local authorities turn over a violent offender, the ICE detainer order gets ignored. According to a local ABC news affiliate, the confessed killer admitted during an interview that he picked San Francisco precisely *because* it is a "sanctuary city."

Within hours of the California killing, a Laredo, Texas, woman was beaten to death with a hammer by her illegal-alien husband. He too, had been previously deported — four times — and the Laredo police admit that they'd had three violent encounters with the illegal alien and his wife. Yet the PD never notified border patrol.

Recall the nearly 60,000 unaccompanied alien children — UACs — that came into the country over our southwest border last year. According to ICE records, nearly 98 percent of the kids are placed with extended family, guardians or foster caregivers in this country, and given a notice to appear before an immigration judge at a future date. As many as 90 percent of the kids never show up. And while the flood of last year has diminished, UACs still come.

The Federation for American Immigration Reform estimates that illegal immigration costs Californians $25 billion per year, when you include the cost of educating children of illegal aliens.

Peter Kirsanow, a black member of the U.S. Commission on Civil Rights, said the commission studied the impact of illegal immigration on urban employment. He said that all commission members — conservatives, moderates and liberals — agreed that porous borders especially threaten the job prospects of those living in urban America. He sent a letter to Congresswoman Marcia Fudge, then head of the Congressional Black Caucus, to ask why little is being done about it. He never heard back.

While Trump unfairly maligned all Mexican illegal aliens, he nevertheless articulates what the polls show: most Americans believe that illegal immigration threatens prosperity and that it changes the American electorate to create more Democrats.

California's Latino Education Crisis

July 16, 2015

The Los Angeles Times headline was cheerful: "It's Official: Latinos Now Outnumber Whites in California." The Times said, "As of July 1, 2014, about 14.99 million Latinos live in California, edging out the 14.92 million whites in the state."

Is this good news or bad news?

The L.A. Times seems to think the former. The article cites the chief demographer for the state finance department who asserts, "A young Latino workforce helps the economy by backfilling retiring baby boomers." Really?

Education professors Patricia Gandara of UCLA and Frances Contreras of University of Washington wrote the 2009 book "The Latino Education Crisis: The Consequences of Failed Social Policies." Heather Mac Donald, a contributing editor of City Journal, reviewed the book. She wrote: "Hispanics are underachieving academically at an alarming rate, the authors report. Though second- and third-generation Hispanics make some progress over their first-generation parents, that progress starts from an extremely low base and stalls out at high school completion. High school drop-out rates — around 50 percent — remain steady across generations. Latinos' grades and test scores are at the bottom of the bell curve. The very low share of college degrees earned by Latinos has not changed for more than two decades. Currently only one in 10 Latinos has a college degree."

Before the book came out, co-author Gandara wrote an article for the National Education Association, where she said: "The most urgent problem for the American education system has a Latino face. Latinos are the largest and most rapidly growing ethnic minority in the country, but, academically, they are lagging dangerously far behind their non-Hispanic peers. For example, upon entering kindergarten 42 percent of Latino children are found in the lowest quartile of performance on reading readiness compared to just 18 percent of white children. By fourth grade, 16 percent of Latino students are proficient in reading according to the 2005 NAEP, compared to 41 percent of white students. A similar pattern is notable at the eighth grade, where only 15 percent of Latinos are proficient in reading compared to 39 percent of whites.

"With respect to college completion, only 11 percent of Latinos 25 to 29 years of age had a BA or higher compared to 34 percent of whites. Perhaps most distressing, however, is the fact that no progress has been made in the percentage of Latinos gaining college degrees over a 20-year period, while other groups have seen significant increases in degree completion."

The New York Times, in 2006, wrote an editorial called "Young Latinas and a Cry for Help": "About one-quarter of Latina teens drop out, a figure surpassed only by Hispanic young men, one-third of whom do not complete high school. Latinas, especially those in recently arrived families, often live in poverty and without health insurance.

"Another piece of the puzzle is how to address the complication of very early, usually unmarried motherhood. Religious beliefs in Hispanic families often limit sex education and rule out abortion. Federal statistics show that about 24 percent of Latinas are mothers by the age of 20 — three times the rate of non-Hispanic white teens. ... One in four women in the United States will be Hispanic by the middle of the century. The time to help is now."

Dr. Anna Sanchez performs deliveries at a hospital in Orange, California, where the mothers are often Hispanic teenagers. She says: "(The) teens' parents view having babies outside of marriage as normal, too. A lot of the grandmothers are single as well; they never married, or they had successive partners. So the mom sends the message to her daughter that it's OK to have children out of wedlock. ... The girls aren't marrying the guys, so they are married to the state."

Married to the state?

City Journal's Mac Donald, in a 2006 article called "Hispanic Family Values? Runaway Illegitimacy is Creating a New U.S.

Underclass," writes: "Hispanics now dominate the federal Women, Infants, And Children free food program; Hispanic enrollment grew over 25 percent from 1996 to 2002, while black enrollment dropped 12 percent and white enrollment dropped 6.5 percent. Illegal immigrants can get WIC and other welfare programs for their American-born children."

"The Latino Education Crisis" authors Gandara and Contreras fear a "permanent underclass." They write, "With no evidence of an imminent turnaround in the rate at which Latino students are either graduating from high school or obtaining college degrees, it appears that both a regional and national catastrophe are at hand."

City Journal's Mac Donald quotes Anita Berry, a case manager who works at Casa Teresa, a California program for homeless single mothers. Berry says: "There's nothing shameful about having multiple children that you can't care for, and to be pregnant again, because then you can blame the system. ... The problems are deeper and wider. Now you're getting the second generation of foster care and group home residents. The dysfunction is multigenerational."

Whether this can be turned around remains to be seen. But it certainly casts doubt on the Times' blissful assertion that "a young Latino workforce (will help) the economy."

Under Obama, Blacks Are Worse Off — Far Worse

July 23, 2015

Ninety-five percent of black voters in 2008 voted for then-Sen. Barack Obama. Surely a "progressive" black president would care about, empathize with and understand black America in a way no other president ever has or could, right? Exit polls from Pew Research show that 63 percent of all voters — and 65 percent of Obama voters — cited the economy as the number one reason they voted for him. Iraq was a distant second at 10 percent. Even for black Obama voters, "It's the economy, stupid."

After six years, the report card is in. The grades are not pretty. By every key economic measurement, blacks are worse off under Obama. In some cases, far worse off.

What about poverty? In 2009, when Obama took office, the black poverty rate was 25.8 percent. As of 2014, according to Pew Research Center, the black poverty rate was 27.2 percent.

What about income? CNNMoney says, "Minority households' median income fell 9 percent between 2010 and 2013, compared to a drop of only 1 percent for whites." The Financial Times wrote last October: "Since 2009, median non-white household income has dropped by almost a 10th to $33,000 a year, according to the U.S. Federal Reserve's survey of consumer finances. As a whole, median incomes fell by 5 percent. But by the more telling measure of net wealth — assets minus liabilities — the numbers offer a more troubling story."

What about net worth and the black-white "wealth gap"? The Financial Times said: "The median non-white family today has a net worth of just $18,100 — almost a fifth lower than it was when Mr. Obama took office. White median wealth, on the other hand, has inched up by 1 percent to $142,000. In 2009, white households were seven times richer than their black counterparts. That gap is now eightfold. Both in relative and absolute terms, blacks are doing worse under Mr. Obama." Remember, these numbers apply to all "non-whites." For blacks, it's worse.

When looking only at "black net worth" — which is lower compared to non-whites as a whole — white households are actually 13 times wealthier than black households. From 2010 to 2013, according to the Federal Reserve, white household median wealth increased a modest 2.4 percent, while Hispanic families' wealth declined 14 percent, to $13,700. But blacks' net worth fell from $16,600 to $11,000. This is an astonishing three-year drop of 34 percent. Investors Business Daily put it this way, "That's a steeper decline than occurred from 2007 to 2010, when blacks' net worth fell 13.5 percent." The black/white "wealth-gap" has reached a 25-year high.

What about unemployment? In 2009, black unemployment was 12.7 percent, and by 2014, it had fallen to 10.1 percent. This sounds like good news until one examines the black labor force participation rate — the percentage of blacks working or seeking work. It's the lowest since these numbers have been recorded.

In a report for the Center for Economic and Policy Research, economist Dean Baker writes, "The drop in labor force participation was sharpest for African Americans, who saw a decline of 0.3 percentage points to 60.2 percent, the lowest rate since December of 1977. The rate for African American men fell 0.7 percentage points to 65.6 percent, the lowest on record. The decline in labor force participation was associated with a drop in the overall African American unemployment rate of 0.5 percentage points to 11.9, and a drop of 0.6 percentage points to 11.6 percent for African-American men." Not good.

What about home ownership? According to Harvard University's Joint Center for Housing Studies, the picture is ugly: "Millions of homeowners, particularly in minority and high-poverty neighborhoods, are still underwater on their mortgages, while millions more renters have been forced to live in housing they cannot afford or is structurally inadequate. And with the ongoing growth in low-income households, housing assistance reaches a shrinking share of those in need. ... Homeownership rates have fallen six percentage points among black households — double that among white households. ... More than 25 percent of mortgage homeowners in both high-poverty and minority neighborhoods were underwater — owing more than their homes are now worth — in 2013. This rate is nearly twice the shares in either white or low-poverty neighborhoods."

The chairman of the Congressional Black Caucus, Rep. Emanuel Cleaver, D-Mo., in 2011, complained about the economic plight of Black America. He said, "If (former President) Bill Clinton had been in the White House and had failed to address this problem, we probably would be marching on the White House." He repeated the statement 12 months later, when black unemployment stood at 14.1 percent: "As the chair of the Black Caucus, I've got to tell you, we are always hesitant to criticize the President. With 14 percent (black) unemployment, if we had a white president we'd be marching around the White House." Rep. Cleaver should start marching because, to use his own words, the problems have not been addressed.

But, hey, the Confederate battle flag is down.

Why Do Bill and Hillary Clinton Still Get a Pass?

July 30, 2015

Donald Trump's ex-wife, Ivana, recently denied a 30-year-old allegation that Donald Trump raped her. The allegation, according to the New York Daily News, stems from the book "The Last Tycoon: The Many Lives of Donald J. Trump" by Harry Hurt III.

The News wrote: "Hurt's 1993 book ... cited a divorce deposition, in which Ivana Trump claimed her then-husband sexually attacked her. ... In a rage, Trump allegedly tore out clumps of his wife's hair, the book claimed, and ripped off her clothes and assaulted her. 'According to versions she repeats to some of her closest confidantes, 'he raped me.' ...

"Ivana Trump herself, in a statement that ended up on the first page of the book, admitted to there having been an ugly night between herself and Trump in 1989, but said she hadn't used the word 'rape' in her deposition literally."

Ivana Trump now says, "The story is totally without merit." She also publically supports her ex for president, describing herself and Trump as "the best of friends," adding, "He would make an incredible president."

Meanwhile, the cover of the current issue of New York Magazine shows pictures of 35 women who have accused Bill Cosby of rape, attempted rape or sexual abuse. In a recently unsealed deposition in relation to a lawsuit filed against Cosby by another alleged rape victim, Cosby admits giving Quaaludes to women he wanted to have sex with.

This raises a question: Why does Bill Clinton continue to get a pass? Clinton was, after all, accused of rape by Juanita Broaddrick. Broaddrick, on "Dateline NBC," claimed that Clinton, then-Arkansas attorney general and gubernatorial candidate, raped her: "I first pushed him away. I just told him 'no.' ... He tries to kiss me again. He starts biting on my lip. ... And then he forced me down on the bed. I just was very frightened. I tried to get away from him. I told him 'no.' ... He wouldn't listen to me."

She further alleges that Hillary Clinton, shortly after the alleged rape, verbally intimidated her, implying that Broaddrick better keep her mouth shut — or else. At a political event two weeks later, Broaddrick claims that Hillary approached her: "She came over to me, took ahold of my hand and said, 'I've heard so much about you and I've been dying to meet you. ... I just want you to know how much that Bill and I appreciate what you do for him.' ...

"This woman, this little, soft-spoken — pardon me for the phrase — dowdy woman that would seem very unassertive, took ahold of my hand and squeezed it and said, 'Do you understand? Everything that you do.' I could have passed out at that moment and I got my hand from hers and I left. ... She was just holding onto my hand. Because I had started to turn away from her and she held onto my hand and she said, 'Do you understand? *Everything* that you do,' I mean, cold chills went up my spine. That's the first time I became afraid of that woman."

The late British left-wing writer Christopher Hitchens, in "No One Left to Lie To," claimed that three women have made "plausible" allegations of rape by Bill Clinton. He gave no further details — and the media have been relentlessly indifferent.

This double standard reached its nadir when Kathleen Willey, a former campaign aide, described on "60 Minutes" an alleged sexual battery committed by Clinton in the Oval Office. Willey, a Clinton campaign volunteer, says that Clinton took her hand and placed it on his aroused genitalia: "He touched my breasts with his hand ... and then he whispered ... 'I've wanted to do this ever since I laid eyes on you.' ... He took my hand, and he put it ... on his genitals." Willey said she managed to push him away.

Feminist Gloria Steinem, right after Willey's appearance, wrote a piece for The New York Times. Clinton, she said, did *nothing wrong*. "Even if (Willey's) accusation are true," Steinem wrote,

Clinton is "not guilty of sexual harassment." Why? Well, Steinem wrote, "(Willey) pushed him away, she said, and it never happened again. In other words, President Clinton took 'no' for an answer."

The late Barbara Olson, in "Hell To Pay," describes Hillary Clinton as the ringleader behind the "nuts or sluts" strategy employed to malign the various women who alleged having had an affair with Bill. Hitchens' book makes a similar claim.

But as to Broaddrick's allegation, apparently only one national reporter, Sam Donaldson, ever asked Bill Clinton about the charge. To Donaldson's question, Clinton said, in effect, talk to my lawyer. As to Hillary, it does not appear that a reporter has *ever* asked her about Broaddrick's allegation.

Bill Cosby is not an ex-president, and his wife is not running to become president. Donald Trump wants the job. Bill Clinton used to be president. His wife wants the job.

Democrats: They're All Socialists Now

August 6, 2915

Socialism, according to Dictionary.com, is defined as: "A theory or system of social organization that advocates the vesting of the ownership and control of the means of production and distribution, of capital, land, etc., in the community as a whole."

Debbie Wasserman Schultz, the chairwoman of the Democratic National Committee, recently appeared on MSNBC's "Hardball with Chris Matthews." Matthews asked, "What is the difference between a Democrat and a socialist?"

Wasserman Schultz laughed, looked stunned, and began hemming and hawing. Matthews helpfully interjected, "I used to think there was a big difference. What do you think it is?" Still, Wasserman Schultz refused to give him a straight answer. "The difference between — the real question," she said, "is what's the difference between being a Democrat and being a Republican."

Matthews tried again: "Yeah, but what's the big difference between being a Democrat and being a socialist? You're the chairwoman of the Democratic Party. Tell me the difference between you and a socialist."

Still, Wasserman Schultz wouldn't answer the question

A few days ago Chuck Todd of NBC's "Meet the Press" offered her a chance for a do-over. He replayed the exchange with Matthews, then asked: "Given that (Democratic presidential candidate) Bernie Sanders is an unabashed socialist and believes in social democratic governments — (he) likes the ones in Europe — what is the difference? Can you explain the difference?"

And again she either could not or would not answer, and wanted to discuss the difference between Republicans and Democrats.

On the one hand, Wasserman Schultz might have refused to answer because she did not want to put her thumb on the scale of the self-described socialist candidate Bernie Sanders or the likely nominee, Hillary Rodham Clinton. No matter what Wasserman Schultz would've said, it would injure one while helping the other.

That's one explanation. But the more likely explanation is simple. There is no real distinction between today's Democrats and socialists. A few years ago Congresswoman Maxine Waters, D-Calif., conducted hearings in which she grilled oil executives for alleged price fixing. She threatened to nationalize their business. Did *any* Democrat speak out against her threat? No.

Newsweek, in 2009, ran a cover story with the headline: "We Are All Socialists Now." Jon Meacham wrote:

"The U.S. government has already — under a conservative Republican administration — effectively nationalized the banking and mortgage industries. That seems a stronger sign of socialism than $50 million for art. Whether we want to admit it or not — and many, especially Congressman (Mike) Pence and (Sean) Hannity, do not — the America of 2009 is moving toward a modern European state. ...

"... If we fail to acknowledge the reality of the growing role of government in the economy, insisting instead on fighting 21st-century wars with 20th-century terms and tactics, then we are doomed to a fractious and unedifying debate. The sooner we understand where we truly stand, the sooner we can think more clearly about how to use government in today's world. ...

"... This is not to say that berets will be all the rage this spring, or that Obama has promised a croissant in every toaster oven. But the simple fact of the matter is that the political conversation, which shifts from time to time, has shifted anew, and for the foreseeable future Americans will be more engaged with questions about how to manage a mixed economy than about whether we should have one."

Polls, too, show that most Democrats are quite comfortable with socialism. A recent poll found 52 percent of Democrats had a favorable opinion about socialism.

Bernie Sanders has always caucused with Democrats, and they are perfectly comfortable with him. He's still a long shot for the Democratic nomination, but he is rising in the polls. If there is a distinction between him and President Barack Obama on anything major, what is it? Both pushed "universal health care." Both oppose the Keystone pipeline. Both believe taxes should be raised on "rich" people. Both believe in the redistribution of income. Obama wants two years of "free" community college. Sanders wants to make college "free" altogether. Both attack "corporate greed" and both belong to the school of economics that says, "you didn't build that."

Andy Stern, then the head of the Democratic Party-supporting Service Employees International Union, said, "I think Western Europe, as much as we used to make fun of it, has made different trade-offs which may have ended up with a little more unemployment but a lot more equality."

That's an acceptable trade-off in today's Democratic Party.

Jack Kennedy, a tax cutter, defended his plan by arguing it would invigorate the economy. He wanted growth and said, "A rising tide lifts all boats." Today's Democrat, like Wasserman Schultz, would deride Kennedy as a greedy *Republican* advocate of "trickle down."

Not News: Unarmed White Teen Killed by Cop; Two White Cops Killed by Blacks

August 13, 2015

The media enthusiastically remind us that it's the first anniversary of the death of Ferguson's Michael Brown, a death that spawned the so-called Black Lives Matter movement.

In a September speech at the United Nations, President Barack Obama said, "The world also took notice of the small American city of Ferguson, Missouri — where a young man was killed, and a community was divided."

Never mind that both a grand jury and the federal Department of Justice exonerated the officer who shot and killed Brown. Never mind that neither the physical evidence nor eyewitness testimony corroborated the assertions that Brown had his hands up or that he said, "Don't shoot."

Never mind that cops, fearing false accusation of racial profiling and police brutality, are increasingly reluctant to engage in proactive policing — to look for suspicious activity in an effort to prevent crime. As a result crime has gone up, particularly in cities with high-profile cases of alleged racial profiling.

Call it the "Ferguson effect."

In New York City a black man, Eric Garner, was killed by police in 2014 as he resisted arrest. A grand jury found insufficient grounds to indict any of the officers involved. Still it became a cause celebre. In New York City, shootings rose 20 percent during the first half of 2015, compared to the previous year.

In Baltimore, Freddie Gray, a black man who resisted arrest, was placed in a police van, slipped into a coma shortly after arriving at the station and died a week later. Days of riots followed and six officers were indicted in connection with Gray's death. During the riots, Baltimore's mayor told the police, as she put it, to give "those who wished to destroy space to do that." Cops got the message. As in New York, they backed off, doing little more than responding to radio calls — no more proactive policing. As a result, Baltimore is experiencing crime levels unseen in decades. Murders have increased 48 percent in the first six months of 2015 — with most of the homicides occurring after Freddie Gray's April 19 death.

Never mind, according to the Centers for Disease Control, police shootings of blacks are *down* almost 75 percent over the last 45 years, while police shooting of whites remained level. And never mind that the media engages in selective concern.

Selective concern?

In just the last two weeks, two cops, who happened to be white, were killed by two suspects, who happened to be black. And an unarmed white teen was killed by a cop.

In Tennessee, Memphis police Officer Sean Bolton approached an illegally parked car, apparently interrupting a drug deal that was taking place inside. The car's passenger got out, engaged Bolton in a physical struggle and shot the officer multiple times. Bolton, a 33-year-old Marine vet who served in Iraq, died at the hospital. After a two-day manhunt, the murder suspect, on a supervised release following a bank robbery conviction, turned himself in.

In Louisiana, Shreveport Officer Thomas LaValley was dispatched to investigate a potential prowler, an armed man reportedly threatening a family member inside a house. When LaValley arrived, he was shot multiple times, and pronounced dead at the hospital. The alleged shooter, wanted on an attempted second-degree murder charge for a shooting three weeks earlier, was captured the next day.

In South Carolina, an unarmed teenager was shot and killed by a cop. Zachary Hammond, 19, was out on a first date when he was fatally shot by a Seneca police officer during a drug bust. His date, who was eating an ice cream cone at the time of the shooting, was later arrested and charged with possession of 10 grams of marijuana. The shooting is under investigation. But the police claim Hammond was driving his car toward the police officer who was attempting to make the stop, an act that resulted in the officer firing two shots, striking Hammond in the shoulder and torso.

The Hammond family wonders why so little national attention has been focused on their son's death. "It's sad, but I think the reason is, unfortunately, the media and our government officials have treated the death of an unarmed white teenager differently than they would have if this were a death of an unarmed black teen," said Eric Bland, the family's attorney. "The hypocrisy that has been shown toward this is really disconcerting. The issue should never be what is the color of the victim. The issue should be: Why was an unarmed teen gunned down in a situation where deadly force was not even justified?"

Why no national outcry? Simple. To the media only the lives of black suspects matter.

Trump Accused of Trashing GOP 'Brand' — By GOP Brand-Trashers

August 20, 2015

Donald Trump stands accused of "trashing the GOP brand" by many of the same GOP politicians and pundits who have no reluctance in "trashing" the most consequential recent decision made by a Republican president — the decision to go to war in Iraq.

When asked a few months ago whether he would have authorized the 2003 war in Iraq, as his brother President George W. Bush did, Republican candidate and former Florida Gov. Jeb Bush first said yes, "I would have." Then, when criticized days later, the younger Bush did a 180: "So here's the deal. If we're all supposed to answer hypothetical questions, knowing what we know now, I would not have engaged. I would not have gone into Iraq." Other Republican candidates — with the exception of Sen. Lindsey Graham — quickly jumped on board the "I wouldn't have gone into Iraq" bus.

Commentator George Will, who calls Donald Trump "vulgar," once robustly supported the Iraq War. He later called it "the worst foreign policy decision in U.S. history."

And *Trump* is hurting the Republican brand? Let's revisit.

After 9/11, 90 percent of Americans expected an Islamic terror strike again within six months to a year. Iraqi dictator Saddam Hussein, against whom we had previously gone to war in 1991, was shooting at the British and American planes patrolling the "no-fly zones." He was sending $25,000 to families of homicide bombers who struck in Israel. He was stealing from the so-called Oil-for-Food Program, doing who knows what with the money. He had attempted to assassinate President George Herbert Walker Bush, and he had used chemical weapons on the Iranians and his own people on Iraqi soil.

George W. Bush sought and obtained a resolution from the House and from the Senate, and got a unanimous resolution from the United Nations that told the dictator to fully and thoroughly declare what he did with his chemical and biological weapons — or face consequences. At that time over 70 percent of Americans supported going to war in Iraq. Two months after the invasion, a Gallup poll found 79 percent of Americans thought the war was justified — whether or not there was evidence of chemical, biological or nuclear weapons — while only 19 percent believed weapons were necessary to justify the war.

Bush retained the same CIA director, George Tenet, who served under Bill Clinton. Tenet assured Bush that this assertion that Saddam possessed weapons of mass destruction was a "slam dunk." All 16 of our intelligence agencies told Bush — at the highest level of probability — that Saddam possessed WMD. The only dissent was over how far along he was in his nuclear weapons program.

After the invasion, Bush sent in weapons hunter David Kay, and later Charles Duelfer, to locate the expected stockpiles. They did not find stockpiles, but both said that Saddam retained the intent and the capacity — waiting only for the expected lifting of sanctions to restart his chemical and biological programs.

Our current director of national intelligence, James Clapper, said that he believes Saddam *did* possess the stockpiles, but "unquestionably" got rid of them during this run-up in an effort to "destroy and disperse" evidence just before the war began. Top Iraqi general Georges Sada says that he helped send the WMD out of Iraq and into Syria via planes and trucks.

The New York Times reported last year that American soldiers were getting sick because of the chemical and biological material they were encountering: "Jarrod L. Taylor, a former Army sergeant on hand for the destruction of mustard shells that burned two soldiers in his infantry company, joked of 'wounds that never happened' from 'that stuff that didn't exist.' The public, he said, was misled for a decade. 'I love it when I hear, oh there weren't any chemical weapons in Iraq,' he said. 'There were plenty.'"

But The New York Times said the chemical and biological materials encountered by the soldiers were not evidence of an "active" chemical and biological weapons program. Active? Who said anything about "active"? The war resolution simply asserted that Iraq possessed these weapons, demanded their dismantling and an accounting of this dismantling.

No WMD?

Army Chief of Staff Ray Odierno, who just retired, only days ago said: "I talked to all the Iraqi generals. They'll tell you there were nuclear weapons. They believed there were. The bottom line is they absolutely believe there were nuclear weapons on the ground. To say we shouldn't have went in there now because we know there wasn't any or we didn't find any, I think is a little bit of hindsight."

In December 2011, President Barack Obama, who had called Iraq a "dumb war" designed to divert attention from George W. Bush's "failing economy," pulled out. He did so after calling Iraq "sovereign, stable and self-reliant," leaving no stay-behind force.

Our American military did its job. Rather than remind the American people of why we went to war — the near-unanimous intelligence and the very real evidence that the stockpiles *were* there — the Republican presidential candidates run from the war like scalded chickens.

But it's Donald Trump who has "hurt the Republican brand"?

Letter to a Friend: 'Harsh Immigration' Is Not Why Latinos Hate Republicans

August 27, 2015

Dear Larry: Geez, I cannot fathom the polls that have Donald Trump leading. Either a lot of Republicans are just frustrated or stupid, or both — and they want a bomb-thrower. Or it is pro-Hillary Clinton Democrats voting in those polls. Trump is ruining the race for the serious Republican candidates and thereby helping Hillary immensely.

Democrats must be loving his clown act. It deflects attention from Hillary's emails. Over time, Trump has donated more money to Democratic candidates than Republican candidates. Does he have any positions other than the one on immigration? At least from the news clips I've seen, I have not heard any. All he does is harp on immigration — building a wall and deporting 11 million people (um, sure) — and says really nasty things about the other Republican candidates. He is just loathsome and seriously hurting the party.

I despair. — Darrell

Dear Darrell: I don't mind that you dislike Trump — so far — but you should at least understand the GOP grassroots anger out there that propels his rise in the polls.

A blunt, P.O.'d talker like Trump strikes a nerve with people who feel like they're falling behind and, more importantly, have been let down by get-along, go-along GOP leaders. These are the Boehners and the McConnells who huff and puff about President Barack Obama and his "out of control" Democratic Party, but by Thursday have moved on to other issues, after having yet again been out-maneuvered by the Democratic Congressional minority.

How did the Iran deal go from being a treaty to an executive initiative, which means that Obama can enact most of the Iran deal on his own and doesn't truly need Congress's approval or disapproval? How did unpopular Obamacare, navigated by clever Democratic Congressional leaders, get rammed down the throats of the American people without a single Republican vote?

How does a proponent of "strict constructionism" like President George W. Bush appoint Chief Justice John Roberts, who votes twice to save Obamacare from the ash heap of history? How, through executive orders, does Obama shield more than 80 percent of an estimated 11 million illegal aliens from the fear of deportation?

How does Obama preside over the worst economic recovery in our lifetime with very little concern, attention, or care from our mainstream "news" media? Where is the outrage from the Republican leadership?

Most folks' incomes have not come back, and their net worth has, at best, been flat over the last seven years. The stock market, boosted through Federal Reserve sleight-of-hand, has disproportionately benefited the top 1 percent.

Meanwhile, the net worth of all non-white families has fallen almost 20 percent since Obama took office. For blacks, it's even worse. The so-called black/white wealth gap is at a 25-year high — with black income down, homeownership down and equity down. From 2007 to 2010, blacks' net worth declined 13.5 percent. But over the next three years — from 2010 through 2013 — it plummeted *another* 34 percent. But allow a black kid to be shot by a white cop and CNN covers it like the first moon landing.

After Mitt Romney's 2012 loss, the GOP put out a postmortem white paper. Its conclusion? Let's "outreach" to Hispanics. After all, they're the fastest-growing voting block, they perceive the GOP as anti-Hispanic, a more "accommodating" immigration policy will attract them, yada, blah, etc. Bull. I live in California. And I will tell you that Hispanics loathe Republicans for many reasons; the GOP's "hostile" attitude toward immigration is way down on the list of anti-Republican grievances.

Hispanics are leftists. Period. They support higher taxes on the rich, believe in an ever-expanding social safety net and believe Republicans are selfish and only care about the rich. To think that a more "welcoming" position on immigration would lure Hispanics to join the GOP is to believe blacks would shift to the GOP if the leadership collectively condemned the Confederate battlefield field flag. Like blacks, Hispanics consider Republicans "racist," and gestures like supporting "comprehensive immigration reform" would be perceived as forced change just for votes. And no matter how "comprehensive" the GOP position on immigration may be, the Democrats' will be more "comprehensive." Can't win.

And for every additional vote lost from the 27 percent of Hispanics who voted Republican in the last presidential race, many more non-Hispanics would vote Republican if the party addressed *their* concerns — more than offsetting any loss of Hispanic votes. Also, let's not assume that Hispanics are as monolithic as are black voters. As Trump points out, unskilled illegal immigration hurts the jobs and incomes of not just unskilled blacks, but unskilled legal Hispanic workers, too.

A lot of Americans feel alienated. They feel that unless you're gay, black, Hispanic or transgender, nobody cares. A recent poll shows that whites feel they are even bigger victims of racism than blacks!

Believe me, it's *not* just about immigration.

So calm down. All is not lost. – Larry

Jorge Ramos: Activist Masquerading As a Journalist

September 3, 2015

One can be excused if he thought he witnessed a heckler, not a reporter, being ejected from a recent Donald Trump press conference.

Jorge Ramos, a so-called "journalist," works for Univision, and has more than two million nightly viewers. He told Trump, "I have the right to ask a question." Trump repeatedly told him to sit down, saying, "No, you haven't been called. Go back to Univision."

He asked Trump the following "question": "You cannot deport 11 million people. You cannot build a 1,900-mile wall. You cannot deny citizenship to children." That was, at best, a series of statements. At worst, it was a rant.

To his credit, Trump invited Ramos back into the press conference. They engaged in a nearly four-minute exchange during which Ramos informed Trump that "no human being is illegal."

Ramos is from Mexico, but came to America in his 20s on a student visa. Some 25 years later, in 2008, he became an American citizen. Question: Did he live for any period of time in America illegally? Is he also a citizen of Mexico? According to a 1997 amendment to the constitution of Mexico, anyone born in Mexico remains a Mexican citizen, even after they become naturalized citizens of another country, including the U.S. Even the foreign-born children of Mexican natives can retain their Mexican citizenship.

Does he vote in both countries? Apparently, yes. Ramos wrote in 2012: "I've never ceased to be Mexican. I have two passports, and I vote in elections in both countries. I'm deeply proud of this privileged duality. The best thing about America is its embrace of diversity. The worst thing about America, of course, is the racist and xenophobic attitudes that tend to emerge now and then."

When Ramos "interviewed" Ann Coulter about her new book "Adios America," he promised her an "honest debate." But he began with the following "question": "Your numbers are wrong." Ramos proceeded to inform Coulter that her assertion that there were 30 million illegal aliens in the country — not the 10 or 11 million that is often claimed — was "wrong." The accuracy of Coulter's number of 30 million is, of course, a legitimate issue. But reporters ask questions. Activists make arguments.

And we thought MSNBC's "journalist" Chris Matthews was bad. Recall after Barack Obama's election in 2008, a gleeful Matthews said, "I want to do everything I can to make this thing work, this new presidency work. ... It is my job. My job is to help this country ... to make this work successfully. This country needs a successful presidency." Ramos makes Matthews look, pardon the expression, "fair and balanced."

Ramos once said, "I finally recognized that I cannot be defined by one country. I am from both countries. It took me many years to make peace with that thought, and that I was never going back to Mexico."

Tell that to President Theodore Roosevelt, who said: "We should insist that if the immigrant who comes here does in good faith become an American and assimilates himself to us, he shall be treated on an exact equality with every one else, for it is an outrage to discriminate against any such man because of creed or birthplace or origin. But this is predicated upon the man's becoming in very fact an American and nothing but an American.

"If he tries to keep segregated with men of his own origin and separated from the rest of America, then he isn't doing his part as an American.

"We have room for but one flag, the American flag, and this excludes the red flag, which symbolizes all wars against liberty and civilization, just as much as it excludes any foreign flag of a nation to which we are hostile. We have room for but one language here and that is the English language, for we intend to see that the crucible turns our people out as Americans, and American nationality, and not as dwellers in a polyglot boarding house; and we have room for but one sole loyalty, and that is loyalty to the American people."

By that definition Ramos is neither an American nor a journalist.

'Black Lives Matter' Movement Getting Blacks Killed

September 10, 2015

Despite the lack of evidence that there is an increase in cops shooting blacks, let alone shooting blacks unlawfully, a few recent killings of blacks by cops has spawned the so-called Black Lives Matter movement. But over the past 45 years, per the Centers for Disease Control, police killings of blacks are *down* 75 percent. What *are* on the increase, year-to-year, are cop killings.

The No. 1 preventable cause of death of young black males is homicide — usually at the hands of other blacks. The primary cause of preventable death among young white males is auto accidents.

Predictably, the Democratic National Committee recently adopted a "black lives matter" resolution. It promotes the phony narrative that blacks remain victims of racism. If Democrats truly want to help, they would rethink their welfare state policies that have decimated black families. In 1950, only 18 percent of blacks were born outside of wedlock. Today, that number is over 70 percent.

Left-wing-driven welfare state policies have incentivized women into marrying the government, and men into abandoning their financial and moral responsibility. Obama once said a kid growing up without a father is 20 times more likely to end up in jail.

Where is the Black Lives Matter movement on that?

In Chicago alone, an average of 35 to 40 people are killed each month, most of them black, almost all by the hands of other blacks. And most of the cases are unsolved! Nationally, in 2013, 90 percent of black homicide victims were murdered by other blacks.

Where is the Black Lives Matter movement on that?

Peter Moskos, associate professor at the John Jay College of Criminal Justice at the City University of New York, extrapolated figures between May 2013 and April 2015 from the website Killed by Police — although he noted that 25 percent of the website's data, which is drawn largely from news reports, failed to show the race of the person killed.

Based on the site's data, Moskos found that roughly 49 percent of those killed by officers were white, while 30 percent were black. He also found that 19 percent were Hispanic and 2 percent were Asian and other races. "The data doesn't indicate which shootings are justified (the vast majority) and which are cold-blooded murder (not many, but some)," Moskos wrote on his blog. "And maybe that would vary by race. I don't know, but I doubt it."

Adjusted to take into account the racial breakdown of the U.S. population, he said black men are 3.5 times more likely to be killed by police than white men. But also adjusted to take into account the racial breakdown in violent crime, the data actually show that police are less likely to kill black suspects than white ones.

"If one adjusts for the racial disparity in the homicide rate or the rate at which police are feloniously killed, whites are actually more likely to be killed by police than blacks," wrote Moskos. "Adjusted for the homicide rate, whites are 1.7 times more likely than blacks (to) die at the hands of police. Adjusted for the racial disparity at which police are feloniously killed, whites are 1.3 times more likely than blacks to die at the hands of police."

Moskos speculates as to an explanation: "1) cops in more minority cities face more political fallout when they shoot, and thus receive better training and are less inclined to shoot, and 2) since cops in more dangerous neighborhoods are more used to danger; so other things being equal (though they rarely are), police in high-crime minority areas are less afraid and thus less likely to shoot."

Year to year, murders in many cities are up. As always, many factors affect the crime rate. But the "Ferguson effect," causing officers to be less proactive, appears to be one of them. Crime is up in places like Baltimore, New York City and Camden, New Jersey, as officers — feeling under siege and falsely accused of racial profiling — have pulled back and arrests are down. NYPD officers Wenjian Liu and Rafael Ramos were literally executed — gunned down while sitting in a police cruiser — by a black man who wrote on Facebook about his anger over the shooting in Ferguson, Missouri.

A piece about Baltimore officers in The Atlantic captures the mood of the city's cops: "The (Fraternal Order of Police) offers a bleaker, though related, rationale for the decrease in arrests: Officers are afraid, its leader says. On the one hand, they're beset by hostile citizens who carefully monitor every arrest, crowding around officers who are just trying to do their jobs and capturing the detentions on camera, lest they turn into another Freddie Gray situation. On the other hand, police are also afraid a prosecutor will haul them in front of a jury. ... They say that they don't know when they might be charged with a crime, just for doing their jobs."

Hillary Isn't Biden's Problem — Obama Is

September 17, 2015

Is Vice President Joe Biden in or out?

Many praised Biden's "honesty" for saying to Stephen Colbert on CBS' "The Late Show": "I don't think any man or woman should run for president unless, number one, they know exactly why they would want to be president, and two, they can look at folks out there and say, 'I promise you, you have my whole heart, my whole soul, my energy and my passion to do this.' And I'd be lying if I said that I knew I was there. I'm being completely honest. Nobody has a right, in my view, to seek that office unless they're willing to give it 110 percent of who they are."

Actually, a completely honest answer would have been, "I'm watching the polls to make sure Hillary Clinton is completely dead, and I'm secretly meeting with donors to insure I'll be the recipient of their money when she implodes."

Biden may think the main issue is whether Hillary Rodham Clinton has sunk far down enough for him safely to jump in. But his problem is more fundamental. A Biden candidacy represents a third term for Obama. For what reason, on what grounds, should Americans give the policies of the Obama administration four more years?

The latest poll of likely voters from Rasmussen Reports found 64 percent think the country is on the "wrong track" and only 29 percent believe it's headed in the "right direction."

As to the economy — the top reason most voters cast their vote — a majority considers America on the "wrong track," reports The Atlantic in its new poll on the "American Dream" conducted with the Aspen Institute. Pollsters found that 75 percent of the general population believe "the American Dream is suffering," and 69 percent thought "obstacles to realizing the American Dream are more severe today than ever." Among the top economic obstacles cited were "personal debt," "lack of economic opportunity" and "cost of healthcare" — a problem Obamacare was supposed to have solved. Also blamed as top obstacles to achieving the dream were "big government," "high government spending," "Obamacare," "excessive government regulations" and "lack of government policies to support economic growth." The biggest problems in America today, said poll respondents, are "healthcare costs" (cited by 29 percent), followed by "national debt" (23 percent), "too much government spending" (22 percent), "unemployment" (20 percent), "illegal immigration" (20 percent) and that "taxes are too high" (18 percent).

According to the Bank of America's annual Small Business Report, as we enter the sixth year of this recovery, only 21 percent of small businesses say they've "fully recovered." According to Karen R. Harned, executive director on the National Federation of Independent Business Small Business Legal Center, small businesses cite, as the primary reasons, lack of sales, taxes and regulations.

As to regulations, Harned writes: "The reason for this is simple — small business owners directly feel the impact of federal regulation in the daily life of their businesses. The small business owner is often the main person in a business who bears the burden of complying with regulations and paperwork requirements. According to a 2010 study, small businesses spend $10,585 per employee on regulation, which amounts to 36 percent more per employee than larger companies spend. ...

"Always entrepreneurial, with a keen focus on the bottom line, the American small business owner looks for ways to minimize the time and money spent on things other than running his or her business. Since many of these regulations wisely exempt the smallest of small businesses, some employers purposefully do not increase hiring because they do not want to have to comply with the regulatory regimes that await businesses that expand to 10, 15, and 50 or more employees."

This presents a dilemma for Biden, as it does for any sitting vice president in an administration with a lousy economy. He must break with Obama, slam the economy and risk being perceived as disloyal.

Or he can ignore the polls and insult the voters by claiming things are great.

Biden, during a speech on the U.S. economy to kick-off a Labor Day march in Pittsburgh organized by the AFL-CIO, did say, "It used to be when productivity went up in America, everybody got to share. The people who caused the productivity increase, they got to share. They got a piece of the action. Something is wrong, folks." But that's as far as he went. He didn't say what was wrong, let alone blame taxes or regulations or offer any policy to address what's "wrong."

This raises Biden's second dilemma. How is this tax-spend-and-regulate Democrat going to differentiate himself from an administration that has taxed, spent and regulated its way to the very "recovery" that Americans describe as on the "wrong track"? Please tell us, Joe.

When Did Calling Obama a Muslim Become a Slur?

September 24, 2015

During Q&A at a Donald Trump town hall event in New Hampshire, a man called Obama a "Muslim." When Trump failed to "correct" him, David Goodfriend, a Democratic strategist and ex-President Bill Clinton staffer, appeared on Newsmax TV calling Trump "a racist bastard."

Memo to the strategist: Islam is a religion, not a race. But Democratic standard operating procedure is as follows: Whenever possible, convert any issue someway, somehow, into an accusation that Republicans are "racist." The tepid economic recovery continues, most Americans believe our foreign policy is on the wrong track and only 21 percent of Americans support Obama's Iran deal. But hey, Republicans are racist.

By the way, when did calling someone a Muslim, whether falsely or not, become a slur? After all, isn't Islam a "great religion of peace," that's been "hijacked by a minority of extremists"? If so, how does calling someone a Muslim become the moral equivalent of hate speech?

Over at CNN, Anderson Cooper — an alleged "journalist" — crossed the line and became a Jorge Ramos-like activist. Cooper indignantly fumed that Donald Trump "doesn't have the guts to stand up to some loudmouth in his own crowd" and set the town-hall man straight. Today, this is what passes for "journalism."

peaking of the supposed Republican belief the Obama's a Muslim, a February 2015 Washington Post blog article cited a survey conducted late last year by YouGov for the Cooperative

Congressional Election Study. That survey found a majority of Democrats do not believe that Obama is a Christian "deep down." The survey asked, "Which of these do you think most likely describes what Obama believes deep down? Muslim, Christian, atheist, spiritual, or I don't know."

According to the survey, only 45 percent of Democrats believe Obama is a Christian at heart, while 26 percent "don't know," 17 percent said he's "spiritual," 10 percent think he's Muslim and 2 percent believe he is an atheist. Added up, this means most *Democrats* doubt Obama's professed Christianity. Apparently, within the Democratic Party, many "racist bastards" reside.

Where was Anderson Cooper during the 2008 campaign? Then-Sen. Hillary Clinton's campaign, as Politico's John Heilemann recently confirmed, stoked Obama-is-a-Muslim-rumors. On "60 Minutes," Clinton was asked whether she believed then-Sen. Obama was Muslim. She replied, "No," and said she takes Obama at his word. But then she slyly added, "There is nothing to base that on — as far as I know." Nudge, nudge, wink, wink.

Speaking of "correcting" those who say false things, where were the media scolds when Hillary Clinton likened Republicans who want to defund Planned Parenthood to "terrorist groups"? Similarly, the media were AWOL when President Obama outrageously likened Republicans, opposed to the Iran deal, to "Iranian hardliners." You know, the ones who chant "death to America" and "death to Israel"?

When will the media get around to "correcting" those who *still* claim George W. Bush "lied" about Iraq War intel? The Associated Press's former Washington bureau chief, Ron Fournier, said President Bush "lied us into war in Iraq." The Associated Press?! About the Iraq WMD Intel, Sen. Harry Reid, D-Nev., called Bush a "liar." New York Times columnist Frank Rich flatly claimed Bush lied about the Iraq war.

They must have forgotten about the Robb-Silberman report from the bipartisan Commission on the Intelligence Capabilities of the United States Regarding Weapons of Mass Destruction. It was set up by Congress to investigate the intelligence on which the Iraq War was based. Yes, the commission concluded that the intelligence reports were wrong, but found no deception. Silberman, in a Wall Street Journal piece, called the continued assertion that Bush misled the nation "not only false, but ... dangerously defamatory. The charge is dangerous because it can take on the air of historical fact — with potentially dire consequences." Yet when pundits, Democrats and even "reporters" like Fournier say Bush lied — crickets from the media.

As to the assumption that Obama is a Muslim, Gen. Colin Powell once said, "The correct answer is, he is not a Muslim, he's a Christian. He's always been a Christian. But the really right answer is, what if he is?"

What if he is?!

It was the current president of Egypt, Gen. Abdel Fattah al-Sisi — not Donald Trump — who called for an Islamic religious reformation and said that "the entire world is waiting" for it. On New Year's Day 2015, before an audience of Muslim clerics and scholars, al-Sisi said: "It's inconceivable that the thinking that we hold most sacred should cause the entire Islamic world to be a source of anxiety, danger, killing and destruction for the rest of the world. ... It's antagonizing the entire world! Does this mean that 1.6 billion people (Muslims) should want to kill the rest of the world's inhabitants — that is 7 billion — so that they themselves may live? Impossible!"

So let's put the Trump-didn't-correct-the-man-who-called-Obama-a-Muslim furor in context. This is merely the latest example of left-wing media hypocrisy, double standards and selective outrage.

Will Stephen Colbert Give Liberals the Ted Cruz Treatment?

October 1, 2015

"The Late Show" host, Stephen Colbert, in an interview with Sen. Ted Cruz, R-Tex., said conservative icon President Ronald Reagan actually raised taxes and signed an amnesty bill. Gotcha! To the delight of his audience, Colbert argued that if Reagan could "compromise" by raising taxes and granting amnesty, why can't the intransigent Republican conservatives of today do so?

For whatever reason, the normally nimble Cruz failed to educate Colbert and his audience that Reagan came to regret the tax hikes of 1982 — the ones that the left reminds us were, as a percentage of GDP, the largest in U.S. peacetime history.

Congress promised $3 in budget cuts for $1 in tax hikes when Reagan signed the Tax Equity and Fiscal Responsibility Act of 1982. A reluctant Reagan signed, agreeing to "a limited loophole-closing tax increase to raise more than $98.3 billion over three years in return for ... agreement to cut spending by $280 billion during the same period." As Reagan later wrote, "The Democrats reneged on their pledge and we never got those cuts." Reagan's former attorney general Ed Meese later called the deal a "debacle."

As to the amnesty deal, Congress promised two things: The borders would be secured, and employers who hire illegal aliens would be prosecuted. Neither was done. Twenty years later, a remorseful Meese wrote: "The 1986 (amnesty) act did not solve our illegal immigration problem. ... From the start, there was widespread document fraud by applicants. Unsurprisingly, the number of people applying for amnesty far exceeded projections. ... Illegal immigration returned to normal levels and continued unabated. Ultimately, some 2.7 million people were granted amnesty, and many who were not stayed anyway, forming the nucleus of today's unauthorized population."

But nice try.

Will Colbert, when he interviews lefties, do the same thing he did to Cruz? Will he use liberal icons to scold leftwing quests about their unwillingness to "compromise"? After all, some big-name Democrats took positions that would be heretical to today's pro-taxes/anti-gun/pro-public-sector-union/pro-affirmative action/pro-choice/pro-big-government/pro-welfare-state lefties:

Taxes: President John F. Kennedy endorsed at tax cut that reduced the top marginal tax rates from 90 percent to 70 percent, a far deeper tax cut than signed by President George W. Bush. In defending his plan, Kennedy sounded positively Reaganesque when he said, "a rising tide lifts all boats." Today they'd call it "trickle down."

Guns: Kennedy said, "Although it is extremely unlikely that the fears of governmental tyranny which gave rise to the Second Amendment will ever be a major danger to our nation, the Amendment still remains an important declaration of our basic civilian-military relationships, in which every citizen must be ready to participate in the defense of his country. For that reason I believe the Second Amendment will always be important."

Affirmative action: Kennedy was against granting privileges based on race: "I think it is a mistake to begin to assign quotas on the basis of religion or race — color — nationality. ... We are too mixed, this society of ours, to begin to divide ourselves on the basis of race or color."

Unions: Franklin Delano Roosevelt opposed public sector unions, today a major supporter of the Democratic Party. Roosevelt wrote: "All Government employees should realize that the process of collective bargaining, as usually understood, cannot be transplanted into the public service. It has its distinct and insurmountable limitations when applied to public personnel management."

Welfare: Roosevelt, the author of the New Deal, expected welfare to be temporary and called long-term welfare a "narcotic": "The lessons of history, confirmed by the evidence immediately before me, show conclusively that continued dependence upon relief induces a spiritual disintegration fundamentally destructive to the national fiber. To dole our relief in this way is to administer a narcotic, a subtle destroyer of the human spirit. It is inimical to the dictates of a sound policy. It is in violation of the traditions of America. Work must be found for able-bodied but destitute workers. The federal government must and shall quit this business of relief."

Abortion: Former President Jimmy Carter said his party never should have become the party of abortion. "I have never believed that Jesus would be in favor of abortion unless it was the result of rape or incest, or the mother's life was in danger. That's been the only conflict I've had in my career between political duties and Christian faith."

Health care: George McGovern, the Democratic Party's 1972 presidential nominee, wanted to loosen restrictions. In 2008, he wrote: "Under the guise of protecting us from ourselves, the right and the left are becoming ever more aggressive in regulating behavior. ... Buying health insurance on the Internet and across state lines, where less expensive plans may be available, is prohibited."

Regulation: McGovern blamed excessive regulation for the bankruptcy of his post-senate small hotel and restaurant, the Stratford Inn: "Many businesses, especially small independents such as the Stratford Inn, simply can't pass such costs on to their customers and remain competitive or profitable."

Will Colbert cite JFK and other Democrats to urge Hillary Clinton or Bernie Sanders to "compromise"?

The Rachel Dolezal-ation of the Oregon Killer

October 8, 2015

Here's the narrative: mass killers are almost always white men. The Daily Kos recently published a piece with this headline: "How come we can't tell the truth about the White Mass Killer Problem?" It asks, "Just what the fracking hell is the matter with all these mass-murdering white people?" Certainly mass killers are almost always men. But they're not almost always white men. Overrepresented? Perhaps. But almost always white? No.

Chris Harper Mercer walked into Oregon's Umpqua Community College and killed nine people, wounding nine more. On a dating site, Mercer, whose father is white and mother is black, referred to himself as "mixed race."

The Los Angeles Times implied that Mercer was white. The Times, in a sub-headline, said he had "white supremacy leanings." The original article said: "A federal law enforcement source familiar with the investigation said, though, that authorities had obtained some of Harper-Mercer's writings, as well as a note he left behind, suggesting that he supported white-supremacist causes and opposed organized religion." The Times later changed the solitary law enforcement source to "two" sources, but added a line stating, "However, he identified as mixed-race on a dating website and lived with his black mother."

As to non-white mass killers, Selwyn Duke, writing in American Thinker, cited a Mother Jones Magazine compilation of data on mass shootings from 1982 through, at the time of Duke's writing, September 16, 2013 — after the Washington Navy Yard murders. Duke wrote:

"Of the last 20 mass killings of that period, 9 were perpetrated by non-whites.

"That would be 45 percent, which exceeds non-whites' 37 percent share of the population.

"Of the last 30 mass killings, 11 were committed by non-whites — right at the 37 percent mark.

"And what if we go all the way back to 1982? We then have 66 mass killings in which the races of the perpetrators were known, and 22 of them, or one-third, were at the hands of non-whites. Note here that America's demographics have been changing, with non-whites comprising only about 20 percent of the population in 1982; thus, if we consider an approximate average non-white population of 28.5 percent during the 31-year period in question, it appears that, again, mass murderers are slightly disproportionately non-white."

This brings us back to Mercer and his race — at least as defined by some major media outlets.

Now President Barack Obama, of course, is regularly described as America's first black president or America's first "African-American" president. His father was a black man from Africa, his mother a white woman from Kansas. Still, Obama is rarely referred to in the media as multi-racial or biracial. The day after his 2008 election, for example, the Associated Press described the coast-to-coast jubilation after "TV news announced the Illinois senator had been elected the first black president."

CBS News, in an article headlined "'Yes We Did': Black Americans Rejoice," wrote: "People danced in the streets, wept, lifted their voices in prayer and brought traffic to a standstill. From the nation's capital to Los Angeles, Americans celebrated Barack Obama's victory and marveled that they lived to see the day that a black man was elected president."

The BBC said: "Democratic Senator Barack Obama has been elected the first black president of the United States, prompting celebrations across the country."

Things got a bit more complicated when George Zimmerman, the Florida neighborhood watchman, shot and killed black teenager Trayvon Martin. At first, media outlets called Zimmerman "white."

The Associated Press wrote: "Martin was black, and Zimmerman was white."

But then, quite inconveniently, media outlets discovered that while Zimmerman's father is white, his mother was born in Peru and raised in Mexico. So CNN and other media outlets decided on "white Hispanic."

American teen tennis star Madison Keyes, with one black and one white parent, says, "I don't really identify myself as white or African-American." But that did not stop Serena Williams, however, from ignoring her preference. "It's good to see another American, another African-American, in the semifinals playing so well," said Williams.

Similarly, golf star Tiger Woods, whose ethnicity includes Caucasian, black, American Indian and Asian, calls himself "Cablinasian." Yet when he won his first master, the media instantly dubbed him the first "African-American" to win that coveted tournament.

It all gets so complicated. But back the Oregon killer.

Again, after the Oregon shooting, most media outlets — if they referred to his race at all — described him as "mixed," as Mercer indicated on the aforementioned dating site. But if Obama, with one black parent and one white parent is "black" or "African-American," why isn't Mercer?

The media are often accused — by the eternally offended crowd — of intentionally "undermining the image of blacks." In fact, nothing could be further from the truth. The media lean over backwards to avoid any hint of anti-black sentiment. In the case of Mercer, a man with one black parent and one white parent, the narrative of mass-killers-are-almost-always-white caused the media great difficulty. But they tried their best.

After all, Rachel Dolezal, the white former NAACP chapter head who pretended to be black, says we're whatever race we think we are.

Ben Carson: Clear and Present Danger?

October 15, 2015

Dr. Ben Carson, now second in most polls for the Republican presidential nomination, naturally finds himself under attack by threatened lefties. GQ published an anti-Carson article with the headline "F—k Ben Carson," except it spelled out the f-word. Comic actor Seth Rogen tweeted "F—k you" to Carson. And a Daily Beast column accused him of anti-Semitism. The columnist cited Godwin's law, which states that debate gets shut down the minute one invokes Nazi Germany to make a point.

Let's deal with them in order.

First, GQ. What incensed the writer was Carson's assertion that he would not have cooperated with the recent Oregon Community College mass killer, and that he would have urged the other would-be victims to rush the shooter. "I would say, 'Hey, guys, everybody attack him. He may shoot me, but he can't get us all.'" said Carson. To the GQ columnist, Carson must be on performance-enhancing drugs: "You are now bearing witness to an arms race of stupid, because stupid is in such high demand from the GOP base at the present moment. Stupid is what gets you attention, and attention is what gets you better polling numbers."

Was Carson outlandish? Didn't President Obama play host at the White House to three Americans who did just what Carson said — rushed in and subdued a terrorist on a French train?

And isn't military veteran Chris Mintz rightfully being called a hero for taking seven shots as he blocked the Oregon killer from entering his classroom?

And didn't those passengers on United Flight 93 force a crash landing in a field outside Shanksville, Pennsylvania, rather than allow the terrorists to reach their ultimate destination — most likely the White House or the U.S. Capitol building?

Second, let's discuss the Canadian import, Seth Rogen. What prompted his profane tweet? Carson said, "The likelihood of Hitler being able to accomplish his goals would have been greatly diminished if the people had been armed." This prompted Rogen's "F—k you, Ben Carson" tweet — no further elaboration offered. The Anti-Defamation League says that guns would have been of little use.

But Independent Institute's senior research fellow Stephen P. Halbrook, author of "Gun Control in the Third Reich," sides with Carson: "Why did they disarm these people — that would be the political enemies of the Third Reich, and that would be the Jewish people — before they did violence on them? There's only one reason. I'm not saying that Nazi Germany would not have been in tyranny, or that the Holocaust would not have happened, but certainly had people had a better means of resistance, the situation might not have been as bad as it was."

Halbrook points to a number of gun control and disarmament actions in Germany that took place just before and during Hitler's rise to power. "And then in 1938," says Halbrook, "in the weeks before Kristallnacht — the Night of the Broken Glass — why did the Nazis order a general disarmament of all of the Jews in Germany? There's only one reason — they could attack them. Some have said that the Kristallnacht was the day the Holocaust began. And that was the day that there were massive, massive attacks throughout all of Germany — burning synagogues, breaking into Jewish houses, vandalizing their businesses. So gun control facilitated the Holocaust. It didn't cause it — there were a variety of factors that made it possible."

Third, this brings us to Godwin's Law. Mike Godwin, a law professor, noted that in online discussions — if they continue long enough — someone is going to make a Nazi comparison. The term has come to mean that when one uses Nazi comparisons or analogies, he seeks to shut down the conversation, stifling debate.

Does this indignation apply to the left?

Democratic mega-donor George Soros once said the George W. Bush White House displayed the "supremacist ideology of Nazi Germany" and that Bush's administration used rhetoric that echoed his childhood in occupied Hungary. "When I hear Bush say, 'You're either with us or against us,'" Soros said, "it reminds me of the Germans."

Former Vice President Al Gore said, "(President George W. Bush's) executive branch has made it a practice to try and control and intimidate news organizations, from PBS to CBS to Newsweek. ... And every day, they unleash squadrons of digital brownshirts to harass and hector any journalist who is critical of the President."

NAACP chairman Julian Bond, in 2004, criticized those controlling the White House and Congress: "(Republicans) preach racial equality but practice racial division. ... Their idea of equal rights is the American flag and Confederate swastika flying side by side." He later said, "The Republican Party would have the American flag and the swastika flying side by side."

Why the hyperventilation over Ben Carson?

He represents a clear and present danger to the left. He counters Dems' narrative that racism remains a major hindrance to black progress. If 20-25 percent of blacks start voting Republican, the Democratic Party is toast. And they know it.

Unleash the hounds!

Hey, 'Black Lives Matter' — Do Black Opinions on Guns Matter?

October 22, 2015

"Gun control advocates," reports Politico, "frustrated by repeated failures to pass even moderate restrictions on gun ownership, are trying to forge an alliance with Black Lives Matter and the criminal justice reform movement in a strategy shift aimed at overcoming the lobbying power of the National Rifle Association."

Democratic presidential candidate Hillary Clinton recently said: "I think that we have to look at the fact that we lose 90 people a day from gun violence. This has gone on too long and it's time the entire country stood up against the NRA. The majority of our country supports background checks, and even the majority of gun owners do."

Clinton's Democratic rival Bernie Sanders echoed: "All the shouting in the world is not going to do what I would hope all of us want, and that is keep guns out of the hands of people who should not have those guns and end this horrible violence that we are seeing. I believe that there is a consensus in this country. A consensus has said we need to strengthen and expand instant background checks, do away with this gun show loophole, that we have to address the issue of mental health, that we have to deal with the straw-man purchasing issue, and that when we develop that consensus, we can finally, finally do something to address this issue."

And President Obama readies yet another executive order for further gun control. "President Obama," writes the Washington Post, "is seriously considering circumventing Congress with his executive authority and imposing new background-check requirements for buyers who purchase weapons from high-volume gun dealers. Under the proposed rule change, dealers who exceed a certain number of sales each year would be required to obtain a license from the Bureau of Alcohol, Tobacco, Firearms and Explosives and perform background checks on potential buyers."

The civil rights movement, writes professor Thaddeus Russell, author of "A Renegade History of the United States," would not have been successful but for access to guns:

"The philosophy of nonviolence as propounded by Martin Luther King Jr. and the civil rights leadership that emerged in the 1950s was a new and exotic concept to black Southerners. Since before Emancipation, when slaves mounted several organized armed rebellions and countless spontaneous and individual acts of violent resistance to overseers, masters, and patrollers, black men and women consistently demonstrated a willingness to advance their interests at the point of a gun. In the year following the Civil War, black men shot white rioters who attacked blacks in New Orleans and Memphis. Even the original civil rights leadership publicly believed that, as Frederick Douglass put it in 1867, 'a man's rights rest in three boxes: the ballot box, the jury box, and the cartridge box.'"

In her book "A Memoir of My Extraordinary, Ordinary Family and Me," former Secretary of State Condoleezza Rice writes about guns and her minister father. In 1963, four little girls were killed in the bombing of a Birmingham, Alabama, black church. "After the first explosion,' writes Rice, "Daddy just went outside and sat on the porch with his gun on his lap. He sat there all night looking for white night riders.

"Eventually Daddy and the men of the neighborhood formed a watch. They would take shifts at the head of the entrances to our streets. Occasionally they would fire a gun into the air to scare off intruders, but they never actually shot anyone.

"Because of this experience, I'm a fierce defender of the Second Amendment and the right to bear arms. Had my father and his neighbors registered their weapons, Bull Connor surely would have confiscated them or worse. The Constitution speaks of the right to a well-regulated militia. The inspiration for this was the Founding Fathers' fear of the government. They insisted that citizens have the right, if necessary, to resist the authorities themselves. What better example of responsible gun ownership is there than what the men of my neighborhood did in response to the KKK and Bull Connor?"

Today, a disproportionate number of gun murders are committed by and on blacks. Blacks are, therefore, uniquely affected by this issue. Have Democratic politicians bothered to ask blacks how *they* feel about more gun control laws?

A new SurveyUSA News Poll of 500 adults in San Diego, California, did just that. It asked, "Should America have more laws concerning guns? Fewer laws concerning guns? Or just about the right amount of laws concerning guns?"

Half of the white respondents — 50 percent — want more gun laws. Only 26 percent of blacks agreed. Twenty-one percent of whites want fewer laws, while 47 percent of blacks want fewer laws. And 25 percent of both groups thought the amount of current laws are just right.

Altogether, 72 percent of blacks felt that our current gun laws were sufficient — or that we needed fewer. Only 46 percent of whites felt the same way.

If black lives matter, what about black opinions on guns?

Hillary Won. America Lost

October 29, 2015

The narrative following Hillary's testimony at Congress' recent Benghazi hearing is clear: Hillary won. She (for the most part) calmly answered all the questions. She nodded approvingly when the Democrats on the committee accused Republicans of engaging in a partisan witch-hunt.

We've come a long way since bipartisan investigations like the Watergate committee that investigated a Republican president, when then-Sen. Howard Baker — the lead committee Republican — asked, "What did (Nixon) know and when did he know it?"

In Hillary Clinton's Benghazi testimony we learned that she immediately called the attack what it was ?? a planned attack on the Benghazi compound. We learned that she told her family this right away, as well as a Libyan official and the Egyptian prime minister.

She told America, however, as well as family members of the four killed, that the Benghazi attack was a spontaneous reaction to a video made by an Egyptian living in America.

We learned that although she was in constant communication with her friend and non-State Department employee, Sidney Blumenthal, none of the more than 600 requests from officials at Benghazi requesting more security ever, according to her, reached her desk.

She gave a heartfelt and indignant story about how she has lost more sleep than all the committee members "put together" over the death of her "good friend" Chris Stevens, the same "good friend" she referred to as "Chris Smith" shortly after the attack.

She was so concerned about Mr. Stevens that, unlike Mr. Blumenthal, he never had her private email address and she had no communication with him at all for the entire time he served as ambassador to Libya.

Now, it is not a crime to lie to the nation. Her husband serves as an example of that proposition. Nor is it a crime to ignore security concerns in Libya in order to preserve, 50-plus days before the 2012 presidential vote, President Obama's re-election talking points: "GM is alive," "Osama bin Laden is dead," and al-Qaida is "on the run."

Nor is it a crime to allow UN ambassador Susan Rice, five days after the attack, to go on the big five Sunday news networks — ABC, CBS, NBC, Fox News and CNN — and push the attack-at-Benghazi-was-due-to-a-video lie.

As far as the investigation is concerned, Hillary defenders could say it was over before it began. House Majority Leader Kevin McCarthy, R-Calif., handed the they're?out?to-get?her crowd a lifeline when he said that the investigation succeeded in lowering Hillary Clinton's popularity ratings — as if that were the committee's goal all along. Then New York Republican Rep. Richard Hanna, not even a member of the Benghazi committee, said, too, that this was all about nailing Hillary.

Lost in all this is the question of whether Hillary broke the law.

Jeffrey Sterling, a former CIA operative, was convicted of violating the Espionage Act for allegedly giving classified information to a reporter. General David Petraeus pled guilty to a violation of the Espionage Act for unlawfully showing classified information to his biographer/mistress.

About the Sterling case, The New York Times wrote earlier this year: "Mr. Sterling is the latest in a string of former officials and contractors the Obama Administration has charged with discussing national security matters with reporters. Under all previous presidents combined, three people had faced such prosecutions. Under President Obama, there have been eight cases, and journalists have complained that the crackdown has discouraged officials from discussing even unclassified security matters."

But remember, we're talking about the Clintons.

During the Monica Lewinsky affair, while President Bill Clinton was being investigated for matters relating to Whitewater, White House/FBI "Filegate" and White House travel office's "Travelgate," Clinton defenders said, "Everybody lies about sex" and "nobody goes to jail for lying about sex." But during that very time, a woman named Barbara Battalino was in federal prison for doing just that. A psychiatrist at a Veterans Affairs hospital, Battalino had an affair with a patient. She lost her job and medical license. The patient later sued for medical malpractice, and told of the affair. Battalino denied it under oath. Charged with perjury in a federal court, she agreed to a plea bargain deal, accepting a $3,500 fine and six months of home detention on one count of obstruction of justice — which she served during the very time Clinton defenders insisted people who lied about sex did no such thing.

Now whether Hillary Clinton gets prosecuted for violating the Espionage Act is about as likely as a sighting of the Loch Ness monster in Times Square.

Much — if not most — of America doesn't seem to care.

After all, if ex-IRS official Lois Lerner will not be prosecuted despite taking the fifth during congressional hearings, and if Al Sharpton can visit the White House over 50 time despite owing nearly $5 million in back taxes and fines, why shouldn't Hillary get a pass?

CNBC Biased? You Don't Say!

November 5, 2015

Question: What did Reince Priebus not know about CNBC — and when did he not know it?

Priebus, chair of the Republican National Committee, sanctioned CNBC's sponsorship of last week's debate. When during and after the debate many of the candidates blasted the moderators for their bias, Priebus said that the moderators created a "hostile environment" and "it was one 'gotcha' question, one personal low blow after the other."

Please. Why the surprise?

After all, CNBC's parent company, Comcast, employs the Rev. Al Sharpton, Rachel Maddow, Chris Matthews — a virtual murderers' row of GOP-haters. Even worse, CNBC senior Vice President Brian Steel, who attended the GOP Colorado debate, held three different positions in the Bill Clinton administration: He served as Vice President Al Gore's domestic policy adviser, worked as deputy assistant attorney general for policy development in the Department of Justice and as associate director in the DOJ's Office of Public Affairs.

But this is par for the course for the left-wing mainstream "news" media:

George Stephanopoulos, aka Clintonopoulos: ABC's website lists him as "ABC News' chief anchor." One of then-presidential-candidate Bill Clinton's top campaign advisers in 1992, Stephanopoulos served in the Clinton administration as White House communications director and as senior adviser on policy and strategy.

Chuck Todd, moderator of NBC's "Meet the Press," worked on Democratic Sen. Tom Harkin's 1992 presidential campaign. His wife, a Democratic campaign strategist and co-founder of messaging and voter contact firm Maverick Strategies and Mail, worked on Democratic Sen. Jim Webb's 2006 Senate campaign.

Erin Burnett, host of supposedly nonpartisan "Erin Burnett OutFront" show on CNN, worked as a "news reporter" at MSNBC. There she once referred to then-President George W. Bush as a "monkey" while covering French President Nicolas Sarkozy's visit to China. With videotape rolling of President Bush flanked by Sarkozy to his left and German Chancellor Angela Merkel to his right, the reporter gushed, "Who could not have a man-crush on that man? I'm not talking about the monkey, either. I'm talking about the other one." Questioned by the show's host, "Who's the monkey?" the reporter clarified, "The monkey in the middle" — meaning President Bush.

Jake Tapper, host of "The Lead" on CNN, started out as press secretary for a Democratic congressional candidate from Pennsylvania, and worked in the same capacity after her election. His wife was previously a staffer with Planned Parenthood.

Matt Lauer is co-host to "The Today Show" on NBC, another property of corporate parent Comcast. The list of Lauer's left-wing slants, questions, and perspectives are too lengthy to catalog. Newsbusters, a website that monitors liberal bias in the media, compiled an extensive list. Here's just one.

Lauer from Baghdad, in 2005: "Talk to me ... about morale here. We've heard so much about the insurgent attacks, so much about the uncertainty as to when you folks are going to get to go home. How would you describe morale?"

Chief Warrant Officer Randy Kirgiss: "In my unit morale is pretty good. Every day we go out and do our missions and people are ready to execute their missions. They're excited to be here."

Lauer: "How much does that uncertainty of (not) knowing how long you're going to be here impact morale?"

Specialist Steven Chitterer: "Morale is always high. Soldiers know they have a mission. They like taking on new objectives and taking on the new challenges."

Lauer: "Don't get me wrong here, I think you are probably telling me the truth but a lot of people at home are wondering how that could be possible with the conditions you're facing and with the attacks you're facing. What would you say to those people who are doubtful that morale can be that high?"

Capt. Sherman Powell: "Sir, if I got my news from the newspapers also, I'd be pretty depressed as well."

This is the current state of American "journalism." President Obama recently chided the Republican candidates for complaining about the CNBC moderators. "Have you noticed that every one of these candidates say, 'Obama's weak, Putin's kicking sand in his face'?" said Obama. "Then it turns out they can't handle a bunch of CNBC moderators at the debate. Let me tell you, if you can't handle those guys, then I don't think the Chinese and the Russians are going to be too worried about you."

Fox News, according to its Sunday host, Chris Wallace, has offered several times to host a Democratic debate. No dice. And one can only imagine Obama or Hillary Clinton agreeing to a sit down with any of the conservative talk radio hosts that Obama and the DNC routinely criticize as coarsening our political dialogue.

Some good, however, will possibly come about because of the slanted CBNC debate. Mike Huckabee was asked whether Donald Trump possessed the "moral authority" to be president. This, as trial lawyers might put it, opens the door for the same question directed at Hillary Clinton. Stay tuned.

Ben Carson's Resume is Fair Game — But What of Democrats' Resumes?

November 12, 2015

The Politico headline was blunt: "Ben Carson Admits Fabricating West Point Scholarship." Except Carson made no such admission. He acknowledged never applying to West Point. But as a top ROTC student in Detroit, there's little question that had he wanted to go to West Point, he could've gotten in.

Technically, West Point offers appointments, and the full tuition is paid for by taxpayers. But even West Point's own website uses the word "scholarship." In any case, Carson went to Yale, and, as such, could likely have gone to any school in the country.

Within hours, Politico changed its headline to: "Exclusive: Carson Claimed West Point 'Scholarship' But Never Applied."

Whether Carson fabricated parts of his bio is, of course, legitimate grounds for media inquiry. But is there any question that Democrats get less media scrutiny than do Republicans? But for Fox News, would the mainstream media have ever been interested in then-Sen. Barack Obama's relationship with his pastor the Rev. Jeremiah Wright, and Wright's anti-American and anti-Semitic statements?

Unfortunately, politicians, like many job applicants, sometimes enhance their personal stories. Rarely are these discrepancies deal-breakers. Consider some on the Democratic side:

Obama claimed, over and over, that his mom, dying of cancer in a hospital in Hawaii, had to fight with her insurance company to pay her medical and hospital bills. Not true. Ex-New York Times reporter Janny Scott wrote a flattering biography of Obama's mom.

The book, however, contained this little bombshell: The sole dispute was over a disability policy issued by his mother's employer. The hospital sent her *medical* bills directly to her insurance company, which paid the medical bills promptly and without dispute.

Obama said Selma inspired his parents to have him: "This young man named Barack Obama ... came over to this country. And he met this woman. ... They looked at each other and they decided we know that, in the world as it has been, it might not be possible for us to get together and have a child. But something's stirring across the country because of what happened in Selma, Alabama, because some folks are willing to march across a bridge. And so they got together and Barack Obama Jr. was born. So don't tell me I don't have a claim on Selma, Alabama." Moving speech, but Obama Jr. was born in 1961, four years *before* Selma's Bloody Sunday march.

Obama, during the 2008 campaign, said he and Mom were on food stamps. But this was not mentioned in his autobiography. And Hawaii doesn't keep records.

Vice President Joe Biden blatantly lied about his grades in 1987, when the then-Senator was a presidential candidate. Alan Lockwood, author of "Barack O'Liberal: The Education of President Obama," writes: "During his 1987 campaign for the Democratic presidential nomination, Biden falsely claimed that he had 'graduated with three degrees from college' (he had one degree), was 'the outstanding student in the political science department' (he was in the bottom 26 percent of his class), had gone to law school 'on a full academic scholarship' (he had no academic scholarship), and had graduated in the top half of his law school class (he was in the bottom 12 percent)."

Presidential candidate Biden also said he was descended from coal miners. But he wasn't — his ancestors never worked in mines.

Hillary Clinton, after meeting Sir Edmund Hillary in Nepal in 1995, told reporters she was named after the famous climber, who was the first to summit Mount Everest. But he did it six years *after* Hillary was born, and he was widely unknown before that achievement.

There remains a no-fly zone over Hillary and former President Bill Clinton regarding Juanita Broaddrick's allegations of rape and intimidation. But for Ben Caron's "lies" — unleash the hounds!

One cannot attribute this to simple Republican whining. The Washington Post ombudsman, Deborah Howell, admitted her paper's 2008 Obama bias. Examining stories from June 4, 2008, when Obama became the presumptive nominee, until Aug. 15, 2008, the Post ran 142 political stories about Obama, compared with 96 about John McCain. As to front-page stories, Obama was 35 to McCain's 13. What about photographs? The Post ran, during this time, 143 pictures of Obama versus 100 of McCain. In the year leading up to the November election, the opinion pages also showed their bias. Howell wrote: "The op-ed page ran far more laudatory opinion pieces on Obama, 32, than on Sen. John McCain, 13. There were far more negative pieces about McCain, 58, than there were about Obama, 32, and Obama got the editorial board's endorsement."

The Washington Times' Kelly Riddell wrote a few days ago: "A mere 7 percent of journalists identify as Republicans, and when they do give money to political campaigns they usually donate to Democrats, lending evidence to Republican presidential candidates' claims that they are facing a hostile audience when they deal with the press."

Scrutiny of Ben Carson's record is, of course, fair game. Just show the same level of interest in the other side of the aisle. Is that too much to ask? Apparently so.

The Paris Attacks and the Rise of ISIS

November 19, 2015

In the wake of the Paris attacks, let's examine the rise of ISIS.

During the last Democratic debate, Hillary Clinton gave this unchallenged "explanation" of why we left Iraq — without a stay-behind force. She said, "I think that what happened when we abided by the agreement that George W. Bush made with the Iraqis to leave by 2011, is that an Iraqi army was left that had been trained and that was prepared to defend Iraq."

But in 2007, President George W. Bush issued this stark warning about a premature pullout from Iraq: "I know some in Washington would like us to start leaving Iraq now. To begin withdrawing before our commanders tell us we are ready would be dangerous for Iraq, for the region, and for the United States. It would mean surrendering the future of Iraq to al-Qaida. It would mean that we'd be risking mass killings on a horrific scale. It would mean we'd allow the terrorists to establish a safe haven in Iraq to replace the one they lost in Afghanistan. It would mean increasing the probability that American troops would have to return at some later date to confront an enemy that is even more dangerous."

President Barack Obama's apologists now say that, well, Obama simply executed the timetable that the Iraqis and President George W. Bush had agreed to before Obama took office — and thus he pulled us completely out of Iraq.

Here are just a few of the holes in this cover-your-ass-and-blame-Bush narrative.

First, since when has Obama felt bound to anything George W. Bush agreed to?

After taking office, Obama immediately reneged on Bush's missile-defense deal with Poland and the Czech Republic. But when it comes to a stay-behind plan for us in Iraq, Bush tied Obama's hands? Please.

Second, former Vice President Dick Cheney, in October 2011, two months before Obama pulled out all the troops, said that the agreement envisioned a negotiation for a stay-behind force: "There was another provision in (Bush's status-of-forces agreement) that's very important, seems to have been ignored, which was that we would also reserve the right to negotiate with the Iraqis on some stay-behind forces. ... They're a new democracy; they're not very well organized yet. I worry that in the rush for the exit here, that we may in fact make it very difficult for them to succeed."

Third, as Max Boot, a senior fellow in national security studies at the Council on Foreign Relations, describes in a 2011 Wall Street Journal piece, Obama — who ran on getting us completely out of Iraq — never seriously tried to negotiate a deal to stay, didn't want one and found any convenient excuse, including blaming Iraq for its intransigence, to leave without a stay-behind force. "The popular explanation is that the Iraqis refused to provide legal immunity for U.S. troops if they are accused of breaking Iraq's laws," wrote Boot. "So why was it possible for the Bush administration to reach a deal with the Iraqis but not for the Obama administration? Quite simply it was a matter of will: President Bush really wanted to get a deal done, whereas Mr. Obama did not."

Fourth, if Bush tied Obama's hands why did so many push him to leave a stay-behind force? Then-Secretary of State Hillary Clinton pushed for a stay-behind force. According to the Daily Beast, "At the time of the negotiations, Clinton's State Department and the Obama White House were not on the same page. ... For Clinton, her State Department senior staff — as well as for top officials at the time, including Defense Secretary Leon Panetta and CIA Director David Petraeus — there was a national security interest in keeping thousands of troops in Iraq."

Army Chief of Staff Gen. Ray Odierno, upon his recent retirement, said that he, too, believes a stay-behind force could've dealt with ISIS: "I go back to the work we did in 2007 (through) 2010, and we got into a place that was really good. Violence was low, the economy was growing, politics looked like it was heading in the right direction. ... We thought we had it going exactly in the right direction, but now we watch it fall apart. It's frustrating. ... I think, maybe, if we had stayed a little more engaged, I think maybe it might have prevented it." Nothing about "hands being tied" by Bush or that Iraq pushed us out.

It's laughable now to hear Bush-hating critics — who opposed the Iraq war from the start, who voted for Barack Obama because he promised to pull us completely out of Iraq — *now* say they actually *wanted* a stay-behind force in Iraq. But the dastardly George W. Bush, who orchestrated a war they considered "dumb," tied their hands and prevented them from staying. Pass the barf bag.

Do the Bush-hating/Obama-protecting critics think Americans are stupid? Don't answer that.

10 Tips to Survive Today's College Campus, or: Everything You Need to Know About College Microaggressions

November 26, 2015

When students protesting "microaggressions" took over an administrative building at Occidental College in California, they issued 14 demands. The school agreed to all except the first, which required the firing of its president. Similar protests took place concurrently at other colleges nationwide.

Occidental's five-day takeover was organized by Oxy United for Black Liberation, led by members of Oxy's Black Student Alliance (BSA) and Coalition at Oxy for Diversity and Equity (CODE). Occidental says the demands they agreed to meet were:

"Promotion of the new chief diversity officer (CDO) position to vice president level.

"Increase budget of the CDO office by 50 percent.

"Allocate $60,000 to Diversity and Equity Board (DEB) to fund programming and provide resources for black and other marginalized students.

"Creation of a fully funded and staffed Black Studies program, a demand the group says 'has not been met for over 40 years.'

"Increase percentage of tenured faculty of color by 20 percent for the 2017-18 school year, and by 100 percent over the next five years.

"Provide funding for Harambee, the student group for black men, which has not received funding in five years.

"Institute mandatory training for all College employees — especially Residential Education, Student Affairs and Campus Safety

— that provides tools to properly assist people from marginalized backgrounds.

"Immediate demilitarization of Campus Safety.

"Immediate removal of LAPD's presence on campus.

"Ensure the continued existence of the Intercultural Affairs office on campus.

"Elimination of the First Year Residential Education program. In its place, restructure Core Studies Program classes to focus on issues surrounding identity, fulfilling its original purpose.

"Hire physicians of color at Emmons Wellness Center to treat physical and emotional trauma associated with issues of identity.

"Meet the demands that CODE made following the arrest of a community member on September 5."

Whew!

On Twitter, I asked a pro-protest Occidental College student to provide a definition of "microaggression." He refused, instead sending a link to a PhD philosophy thesis on the subject. Repeat, a PhD *philosophy* thesis. The paper's definition:

"The overt nature of racism in the United States has morphed into an insidious, covert manifestation called racial microaggression. ... Though not often intentional in nature, these microaggressive behaviors have become pervasive in the lives of people of color. ... Extant research reveals the harmful and cumulative effects of racial microaggressions. ... Much research has been done on people of color's experiences with racial microaggressions; however, few studies have given attention to why some African American college students are able to excel in microaggressive academic environments while others do not." Oh.

The thesis's author conducted a study with 47 undergraduates, but only 35 completed the survey and were included in the data: "As a result of insignificant results, as well as predominantly male participants, secondary analyses were conducted based on demographic variables, which are salient for African American male college students." Oh.

The paper's takeaway: "Results indicated that students' backgrounds impact how they handle microaggressive behaviors." Seriously?!?

Here's what's really happening.

Faculty leftists now rule the humanities departments in America's colleges and universities. They teach victimhood. Students learn that they've been victims of America's racism, sexism, homophobia, etc. So why the surprise when they begin to *act* like victims? And due to self-imposed or external pressure to "diversify" campuses by race and ethnicity, colleges relax customary academic standards of admission for so called "underrepresented students," specifically blacks and Hispanics. Such students would have done fine at a less competitive school, one commensurate with their grades and test scores. But when standards are watered down, students can struggle to compete, thus becoming "academically marginalized." Thus the very same students who "benefited" from the push for diversity then complain about the perceived "microaggressions" that supposedly hinder their success.

So, given anti-microaggression protests at places such as Dartmouth, Brown, Columbia, Occidental and University of Missouri, among others, we offer 10 Tips to Survive Today's College Campus, or: Everything You Need to Know About College Microaggressions:

1. Facts are "microaggressions."

2. Facts are racist.

3. Blacks cannot be racist. Racism requires power. Blacks lack power and therefore cannot be racist.

4. A student of color, except for Asians, who gets bad grades is "academically marginalized."

5. Professors who give bad grades to students of color, except for Asians, are racists.

6. The SAT is culturally biased.

7. White male students/staff/faculty must renounce their "white male privilege" and then, well, we'll get back to you on that.

8. If you're white and your response to "Black Lives Matter" is that "All Lives Matter," you're a racist.

9. If you're black and your response to "Black Lives Matter" is that "All Lives Matter," you're an "Uncle Tom."

10. If you're Latino and your response to "Black Lives Matter" is that "All Lives Matter," you're a "Tio Taco."

Good luck.

Chicagoland: A Tale of 2 Tragedies

December 3, 2015

In October 2014, 17-year-old Laquan McDonald was shot and killed by Chicago Police Officer Jason Van Dyke.

The dash-cam video of the shooting was not released until a few days ago, when ordered by a judge. Right before the video's release, the county prosecutor announced the intention to charge Van Dyke with first-degree murder. The excessive charge and the timing were done, presumably, to mollify potential protesters because the prosecutor called the investigation "ongoing."

Following the release of the video, which showed McDonald being shot 16 times, protesters marched on Chicago's Michigan Avenue (aka the "Magnificent Mile") on Black Friday, inconveniencing shoppers — even barring them from entering and leaving some prominent stores — and causing retailers to lose money on the year's most important shopping day.

Four weeks ago, the Chicago Tribune reported that three gang members lured a nine-year-old from a park and into an alley, then executed him, allegedly as an act of revenge against the boy's father, for his ties to a rival gang. "After his brother and his mother were shot," reported the Tribune, "Corey Morgan, 27, and two other Terror Dome (gang) members had driven around on a daily basis looking for revenge, prosecutors have alleged. Morgan vowed to kill 'grandmas, mamas, kids and all,' they said.

"The three found their target on a warm Nov. 2 as 83-pound Tyshawn (Lee) played in Dawes Park near his grandmother's Auburn Gresham home, prosecutors said. One of the three chatted up Tyshawn, walked with him to the alley and then shot him five times as Morgan and the third individual looked on from a black SUV, prosecutors charged. Police found Tyshawn's beloved basketball near his body. Superintendent Garry McCarthy said the boy was targeted because of his father's gang involvement."

If anybody marched on the Magnificent Mile to protest yet another Chicago killing — this time the cold-blooded murder of nine-year-old Tyshawn — the media failed to notice.

As for police shootings, in 2014, Chicago cops killed 17 people. This year, with one month to go, Chicago cops have killed seven.

On the other hand, Chicago — so far — has seen almost 450 homicides, mostly black on black, and mostly involving young blacks. Incredibly, only 25 percent or so are solved.

True, in 2014, of the people fatally shot or wounded by Chicago cops, 78 percent were black. But it is equally true that of all Chicago homicides in 2014, 78 percent of victims were also black. And for young black men, homicide — usually committed by other young black men — is the No. 1 preventable cause of death. For young white men, it's automobile accidents.

As for 17-year-old McDonald, The Associated Press describes a kid raised without a father, shuttled around by the child services system: "A black teenager shot 16 times by a white Chicago police officer was a ward of the state when he died, having spent years being shuttled between different relatives' homes and foster care from the time he was 3. ...

"McDonald, (who) grew up without his father involved in his life ... spent most of his 17 years as a ward of the state. According to Illinois Department of Children and Family Services' records, he was taken from his mother at age 3 in 2000 because the agency had deemed that his mother didn't provide him with proper supervision. He was placed in a foster home.

"He later moved to his great-grandmother's, and returned to his mother in 2002. But citing physical abuse by the mother's then-boyfriend, the state again took McDonald away. From around age six to 16, he lived with his great-grandmother and then stayed in the same house with an uncle after his great-grandmother died in 2014."

That McDonald died at the hands of an officer is rare. Sadly, the way McDonald was raised — without a father and without appropriate parenting — is all too common.

Meanwhile, Chicago Mayor Rahm Emanuel has fired Police Superintendent Garry McCarthy. And, yes, this is the same

McCarthy who, along with Mayor Emanuel and a principal of an urban high school, was portrayed as a hero in a 2014 CNN reality TV series called "Chicagoland."

When Ferguson's Michael Brown and Baltimore's Freddie Gray were killed by police, Department of Justice probes began within days. Chicago's Laquan McDonald was killed in October 2014, but the DOJ probe didn't start until April 2015. Mayor Rahm Emanuel, of course, is Obama's ex-chief of staff.

A killing by a cop causes "activists" to hit the streets. But a black nine-year-old targeted and killed by three black gang members — no march. What about agitating against a welfare state that encourages women to marry the government — and men to abandon their financial and moral responsibilities?

Wishing Terrorism Away

December 10, 2015

When asked why President Barack Obama insisted on pursuing a nuclear deal with Iran, former Secretary of Defense Robert Gates said: "I think that the pursuit of the agreement is based on the President's hope that over a 10-year period with the sanctions being lifted that the Iranians will become a constructive stakeholder in the international community. That — that as their economy begins to grow again, that — that they will abandon their ideology, their theology, their revolutionary principles, their meddling in various parts of the region. And, frankly, I believe that's very unrealistic."

The very morning of the Paris attacks, Obama called ISIS/ISIL "contained." And hours before last month's al-Qaida-claimed hotel attacks in the capital of Mali, Africa, which killed 20, Secretary of State John Kerry pronounced al-Qaida "neutralized."

Even after the Paris attacks, Obama summoned only enough indignation to describe the attacks as a "setback." Meanwhile, the equally leftist, equally anti-war French president Francois Hollande called the attacks an "act of war," and promised, "France, because it was foully, disgracefully and violently attacked, will be unforgiving with the barbarians from Daesh (ISIS)."

Just as he did following the deadly attack at a Colorado Planned Parenthood clinic, Obama, after the radicalized Islamic-inspired terror attacks in San Bernardino, California, called for more gun control. He also urged Congress to pass laws preventing those whose names appear on a no-fly list from acquiring firearms, as well as other "common sense" measures.

Never mind that California, where the two radical Islamists murdered 14 and wounded 21, long ago imposed "common sense" measures, including the closure of the so-called "gun-show loophole," restrictions on the purchase of certain assault and assault-style weapons, limits on handgun purchases to one per month per person and a 10-day waiting period prior to the sale or transfer of a firearm.

The New York Times echoed Obama by running its first front-page editorial since 1920. Did the Times call for U.S. ground troops in the Middle East, a measure that polls now show a majority American support? Did the editorial demand imposing a no-fly zone in Syria? Or demand changing the rules of engagement to loosen the concern of "collateral damage" — which many military experts believe severely hampers us from defeating ISIS? Did the Times ask Obama rethink the plan to bring in tens of thousands of Syrian refugees? (After all, the Pakistani-born San Bernardino killer/mother immigrant had supposedly been vetted. And as to Obama's assurance that Syrian refugee mothers and their children pose no threat, Tashfeen Malik left behind her 6-month-old daughter as she and her husband left the house to go on a murder spree.)

No, the Times, in its first front-page editorial in almost 100 years, demanded more control laws. Goodness, if it's that simple, why not just demand that Iraq and Syria enact "common sense" gun-control laws, thereby putting ISIS out of the war business? No weapons, no war.

Polls show that most Americans either believe President Obama has no idea how to combat ISIS, or feel that the terror group is gaining strength. That assessment was corroborated by the chairman of the Joint Chiefs of Staff, Marine Gen. Joseph Dunford, who, days after the Paris attacks, told Congress, "We have not contained ISIL (ISIS)."

Due to mounting criticism, Obama gave a rare, televised Oval Office Sunday night speech designed to assure the nation that everything that can be done is being done, and that ISIS' days are numbered. But he announced no new initiatives, gave no hint of possibly committing combat troops.

Obama and his would-be successor, Hillary Clinton, focus more anger at Republicans than at the terrorists. After the Paris attacks, Obama scolded Republicans for wanting restrictions on Syrian refugees. And Clinton compared Republicans seeking to defund

Planned Parenthood to "terrorist groups." She likened NRA supporters to "Iranians or the communists."

Obama is the same commander in chief who failed to negotiate a stable force in Iraq; who pulled out all the troops in Iraq over the objections of his then-Secretary of Defense Leon Panetta, his Secretary of State Clinton and his former Chairman of the Joint Chiefs of Staff Martin Dempsey; who once called ISIS a "JV team"; and who, again, the morning of the Paris attacks, called ISIS "contained." But Obama *now* claims to have adopted the right strategy to defeat a terror group even as he still refuses to utter the phrase "radical Islam."

Some argued that future historians would rehabilitate the reputation of George W. Bush, who left office as one of our most unpopular presidents. Well, the future is now. A June 2015 Gallup poll found that the number of Americans who call the Iraq War a "mistake" declined from 57 percent in 2014 to 51 percent a year later. And this was before the attacks in Paris, Mali, Lebanon and San Bernardino, all of which occurred in a span of three weeks.

But those angry at President Obama for his limp Sunday address should stand down. After all, when was the last time Obama gave a major national security speech without mentioning "climate change"?

A Hollywood Christmas Story

December 17, 2015

The following story is true. The names have been changed to protect the innocent.

I drove past the outdoor parking-lot-turned-Christmas-tree-store several times before I decided to buy my Christmas tree from there. It was fairly close to my home in the Westside of Los Angeles, and business seemed brisk. Must be a nice place.

Soon I found a nice, fluffy, well-shaped tree. "How much?" I asked a smiling salesman. "$60," he said, showing me the price tag I had overlooked, "Good deal." Then he said, "Are you Larry Elder? Big fan." "Guilty," I said. "Is this your place?" "No," he said, "I'm an actor, just doing this part-time to make a few bucks for the holidays."

I'm always surprised when I meet non-left-wing actors, a rare breed in this town — especially those out of the closet. I asked how his career was going. "Mark" told me the names of a few TV shows and movies in which he'd appeared.

But lowering his voice, he said, "When you're a Republican in this place, it gets tough." He told me about jobs he felt he'd lost because someone told someone that he was "a Republican." "I'm not even sure I am," he said, lowering his voice still more. "But I know we can't handle four years of Hillary."

Soon, another salesman came over, also an actor and fan of my show. "Tommy" said, "I'd ask you what you think about the Republican field, but you're not working, right?" We all laughed. "I'm just here to buy a tree," I said.

Believe it or not, a third person, shopping for a tree, overheard the conversation. She came over. She, too, enjoys my show, but said:

"It's caused a rift between friends and even family members. Oh, they're tolerant and caring — as long as you agree with them." The shopper, "Sandra," it turns out, was also an actor.

Well, now the four of us started exchanging stories of left-wing intolerance, practically completing each other's sentences.

Sandra told us about an acting gig in the home of a well-known comedian for some online video. When Sandra found out, because of some offhand comment, that the comedian was also a conservative, they started talking — only to be to be interrupted by the cameraman who complained about their "right-wing crap." Sandra said, "(The comedian) reminded him that, one, this was *her own home* and, two, *she* hired *him*, and then the cameraman finally shut up."

I told a story I once heard about actor Ed Asner. "On the set of 'Lou Grant,'" I said, "Asner said he never hired anyone who voted for Ronald Reagan. Publicly said it!"

I told them about the time a movie was filmed at the house next door to mine. The film's location scout negotiated with me to use my driveway and patio area for parking and catering.

During the filming, I stood on my porch and watched them shoot some takes. The caterer came over to me, said he enjoyed my show, and we talked for 15 to 20 minutes.

Months later, the same caterer called my radio show. He said when people observed him speaking with me, "The word spread that I must therefore be a Republican. Haven't worked on a shoot since."

After a few minutes swapping stories, a man yelled from a booth on the tree lot and told Mark and Tommy to "get back to work." As they scattered, Mark pointed to the booth and whispered, "He's the owner. When I told him you were here, he said, 'And you're impressed by *that* guy?'" I laughed, "Not a fan." He shook his head. "Occupational hazard," I said, "I just hope he doesn't jack up the price on me." We laughed.

I looked around for several more minutes, making sure that I was getting the best tree for the size and shape I wanted. But I settled on the one I first liked.

"$80," said the owner. I handed him my credit card, and signed the receipt before recalling that Mark told me it was $60. Maybe, I thought, I misheard Mark. But then I remembered being shown the $60 tag.

So I found Mark, and told him that his boss charged me $80. Angry, he told me to wait and stormed over to the booth. The boss and he had an animated exchange. I couldn't hear what was said, but I was refunded $20.

After two workers tied the tree to the top of my car. I found Mark, put my arm around him and thanked him for intervening. "But I better get out of here while you still have a job."

Mark didn't disagree. But he smiled, "This town. Merry Christmas."

15 Questions in Search of a Democratic Debate

December 24, 2015

1) Polls show that, by a large margin, Americans feel we're on the wrong track, both economically and as to foreign policy. Yet none of you offers *any* criticism of President Barack Obama, who has been in charge for the last seven years. Why, then, should Americans believe that four more years, under your leadership, would be any different from the last seven?

2) Sen. Sanders, you've called for a $15-per-hour minimum wage. But even Vice President Joe Biden's economist, Jared Bernstein, considers a $15 hourly rate so high that it would cause an unacceptable loss of jobs. Is he wrong?

3) Secretary Clinton, you advocate "debt-free tuition," and Sen. Sanders, you want free universal health coverage and paid family medical leave. You both say that you can accomplish this by raising taxes on the rich. But isn't it true that if you completely confiscated the earnings of the top 1 percent, you couldn't fund the current obligations of the federal government, let alone the new programs you want?

4) Sen. Sanders, you blame the 2007-2008 economic crisis, in part, on the removal of a part of Glass-Steagall, a 1933 depression-era regulation that prevented banks from engaging in both traditional banking and investment banking. President Bill Clinton is the one who got rid of it. He still stands by that decision, and believes it had nothing to do with the Wall Street/banking meltdown. Why is he wrong, but you are right?

5) Secretary Clinton, you described the higher premiums and higher deductibles — under Obamacare — as "glitches." But don't these "glitches" mean that Obamacare is failing to realize many of its objectives?

6) United Healthcare, the nation's largest insurer, says its past support for Obamacare was a mistake, is losing money under Obamacare, and now says it may pull out altogether. Again, doesn't that say that Obamacare is failing to achieve its main objectives?

7) Secretary Clinton, the U.S. joined with the French and the British in bombing Libya to depose Moammar Gadhafi. You've justified this by noting he was a tyrant and his departure meant that Libya could have free elections. Wasn't Saddam Hussein of Iraq a tyrant, and didn't the Iraqis have free elections after he was deposed by our invasion? Why is Libya OK, but Iraq a foreign policy blunder?

8) You've all criticized the Iraq war as a blunder because President George W. Bush ignored the unintended consequences of deposing a strong man who held the country together. Didn't President Jimmy Carter do the same thing when he pushed the shah of Iran to release what Carter called "political prisoners" — which we now call radical jihadists? This led directly to the current Islamic Republic of Iran. Does Jimmy Carter get a pass for *his* nation building because he is a Democrat?

9) You've all denounced "institutional racism." But President Obama, the first elected black president, has been in charge for seven years. Does he bear any responsibility for the persistence of institutional racism? And why do polls show that race relations, under this president, are the worst in 20 years?

10) Obama has said, "Children who grow up without a father are five times more likely to live in poverty and commit crime; nine times more likely to drop out of schools and 20 times more likely to end up in prison." As between "institutional racism" or the breakdown of the black family, isn't the breakdown of the family a much bigger problem when over 70 percent of black children are born without a father in the house?

11) All of you support the "Black Lives Matter" movement that has given support to college students who complain about so-called "microagggressions." To fight microaggressions, some students want

a campus "safe space." What is the difference between a "safe space" and segregation?

12) All of you have denounced Donald Trump as a racist, a bigot and a fascist. But in 1993, Sen. Harry Reid sounded Trump-like when he introduced a bill to end birthright citizenship; advocated restrictions on legal immigration and on asylum-seekers; and wanted stiffer penalties for visa fraud. If Trump's a bigot, isn't Harry Reid?

13) Sen. Sanders, you say a police department should "look like the community they are policing." But in Baltimore — where Freddie Gray died in a police van and where Gov. O'Malley was mayor from 1999 until 2007 — the majority of cops are people of color, the former PD head was black and the police command staff is majority black. What does this tell us?

14) Secretary Clinton, you've said that as to the allegations of sexual assault, women should be believed. Is this applicable to Juanita Broaddrick, Kathleen Willey and Paula Jones?

15) According to the Pew Research Center, 91 percent of Muslims in Iraq and 84 percent of Muslims in Pakistan support sharia law. Yet Iraq and Pakistan are the top two green card countries for the United States. Isn't this both an assimilation problem and a national security problem?

Hey, NFL, What About the Taxpayers' Concussion?

December 31, 2015

Three NFL teams claim they want to come to Los Angeles, the nation's second-biggest market. Their current home cities either did not agree to build a taxpayer-funded stadium or are dragging their feet in doing so.

Now each of the possibly L.A.-bound teams *used* to play in L.A., before they left for greener pastures — aka more taxpayer money than L.A. offered. The two competing L.A. stadiums, where a team or two might or might not be playing, *supposedly* are being built (or will be built) without tax dollars: one in L.A.-adjacent Inglewood, the other in nearby Carson.

The teams are:

The Oakland Raiders, who actually left their birth city of Oakland, played in L.A. for a few seasons and then returned to Oakland when those taxpayers ponied up. Raiders' owner Mark Davis says he prefers to stay in Oakland, even as he confabs with the San Diego Chargers (more about them later) on a deal to share a new stadium to be built in Carson. Davis says the Raiders have $500 million to put into a new Oakland stadium — $300 million from the team and another $200 million from an NFL loan program — but insists that Oakland needs to put in $400 million or so to get a $900 million stadium built.

The St. Louis Rams, who *used* to play in Los Angeles for decades before the "Show Me State" taxpayers and politicians lured them to Missouri with a new stadium and amenities for which they'll *still* be paying if and when the Rams move. Like the Raiders, St.

Louis now demands a new stadium for them to stay. St. Louis recently offered to pony up $150 million for a new stadium. That offer requires the NFL to put $300 million into the pot — and the NFL will only commit to $200 million.

The San Diego Chargers used to play in L.A. when the team began as the Los Angeles Chargers in the old American Football League that eventually merged with the NFL. To remain in San Diego, the Chargers also want a new stadium, but the city is mired down in environmental impact studies, challenges for funding and finagling tax revenues. The team already nixed an offer by the city for a downtown location, in part because the hotel industry didn't "offer" the Chargers anything to support that deal.

Why taxpayers give the already massively rich owners their tax money — only to be jilted if they don't do it again in 20 or 30 years — is worthy of a taxpayer-funded study. They shower tax subsidies and other public concessions on multibillionaire owners who pay multimillionaire players, all of which the decidedly non-wealthy fans end up paying. Nearly every stadium — via taxpayer money — gives owners grants, tax forgiveness, tax abatements, parking and refreshment concessions, sweetheart deals, free or below-market rent or some combination of all of the above.

Later, when owners demand that taxpayers pony up a spiffy new $600 million stadium with a retractable sunroof and luxury boxes, they truck down to city council and say, "Ante up, or I call the movers!" There's always another Suckersville, with an ego-driven but economically illiterate mayor willing to open the vault and yell, "Come on down!"

Politicians tell their constituents that taxpayer-financed stadiums and arenas generate jobs and attract revenue. But Charles C. Euchner, author of "Playing the Field," a book about cities' bidding wars for sports teams, points out, "Money spent on stadiums is money not available for other infrastructure projects, and most U.S. cities are in a state of crisis regarding the condition of roads, water and sewer mains, bridges and tunnels and subways."

Tax subsidies and tax breaks guarantee profits for team owners. And if, despite this generous cushion, owners go bust (or say they do), cities line up to enrich them at taxpayer expense, only to get stiffed when another town blows them kisses.

When other businesses face revenues that are "not sufficient to the economics," they downsize, cut costs or shut down money-losing operations. But when it comes to sports franchises, let's call this what it is — massive, inexcusable corporate welfare, a shakedown that massively rips off taxpayers.

The movie "Concussion" depicts an NFL supposedly concealing evidence of the long-term brain damage from the head trauma experienced by players. Where's the film on the pocketbook trauma experienced by the taxpayers misled about the alleged, but non-existent, financial benefits of taxpayer-built stadiums? To the owners, it's a business. To the players, it's a job. It's only to the fans that it's a loyalty-driven passion.

So, fans, bend over and cough.

About the Author

A "firebrand libertarian" according to Daily Variety, best-selling author, radio and TV talk show host Larry Elder has a take-no-prisoners style, using such old-fashioned things as evidence and logic. Larry shines the bright light of reasoned analysis on many of the myths and hypocrisies apparent in our system of government, our society, and the media itself. He slays dragons and topples sacred cows using facts, common sense and a ready wit.

Larry hosted, for 15 years, the longest-running afternoon drive-time radio show in Los Angeles, beginning in March 1994. "The Larry Elder Show," a top-rated daily program from 3 p.m. to 7 p.m. on KABC 790, became a nationally syndicated daily talk show for ABC Radio Networks on Aug. 12, 2002. Now Larry is seeking airwave dominance over the morning hours, broadcasting from KABC from 9 a.m. until noon. Known to his listeners as the "Sage From South Central," Larry sizzles on the airwaves with his thoughtful insight on the day's most provocative issues, to the delight, consternation and entertainment of his listeners.

In his best-selling book "The 10 Things You Can't Say in America," Larry skewers the crippling myths that dominate the public agenda. Larry punctures all pretension, trashes accepted "wisdom" and puts everyone on notice that the status quo must be shaken up. In his second book, "Showdown: Confronting Bias, Lies and the Special Interests That Divide America," Larry again takes on the Nanny State, "victicrats" and the politically correct. His latest book, "What's Race Got to Do with It? Why it's Time to Stop the Stupidest Argument in America," is being praised as an important, groundbreaking must-read for the future of race relations in

America. Elder also writes a nationally syndicated newspaper column, distributed through Creators Syndicate.

Larry was also host of the television shows "Moral Court" and "The Larry Elder Show." Larry created, directed and produced his first film, "Michael & Me," a documentary that examines the use of guns in America.

~~~

DOUBLE STANDARDS: THE SELECTIVE OUTRAGE OF THE LEFT
is also available as an e-book
for Kindle, Amazon Fire, iPad, Nook and
Android e-readers. Visit
creatorspublishing.com to learn more.

o o o

CREATORS PUBLISHING

We publish books.
We find compelling storytellers and
help them craft their narrative,
distributing their novels and collections
worldwide.

o o o